Defoe Abbott Marx Hardy Machiavelli Montaigne Chesterton Cooper Emerson Joyce Austen Hugo Eliot Grimm
Melville Haggard Molière
Stoker Carroll Christie Maupassant Byron Schiller Wilde
Garnett Engels Smith Kafka Hall
Goethe Einstein Fitzgerald Hawthorne Dostoyevsky Kipling Doyle Willis
Cotton Henry Nietzsche
Baum Leslie Dumas Flaubert Turgenev Balzac
Stockton Vatsyayana Crane
Burroughs Verne Vinci
Curtis Tocqueville Whitman Gogol Busch
Homer Widger Tolstoy
Darwin Thoreau Twain Scott Plato Harte
Potter Freud Zola Lawrence Dickens Burton Hesse
Kant Jowett Stevenson Cervantes
Andersen Voltaire Cooke
London Descartes Wells
Poe Aristotle Burton
Hale James Hastings
Bunner Shakespeare Irving
Richter Chekhov Chambers da Shaw
Doré Dante Swift Wodehouse Benedict Alcott
Pushkin
Newton

 tredition®

tredition was established in 2006 by Sandra Latusseck and Soenke Schulz. Based in Hamburg, Germany, tredition offers publishing solutions to authors and publishing houses, combined with world-wide distribution of printed and digital book content. tredition is uniquely positioned to enable authors and publishing houses to create books on their own terms and without conventional manu-facturing risks.

For more information please visit: www.tredition.com

TREDITION CLASSICS

This book is part of the TREDITION CLASSICS series. The creators of this series are united by passion for literature and driven by the intention of making all public domain books available in printed format again - worldwide. Most TREDITION CLASSICS titles have been out of print and off the bookstore shelves for decades. At tredition we believe that a great book never goes out of style and that its value is eternal. Several mostly non-profit literature projects provide content to tredition. To support their good work, tredition donates a portion of the proceeds from each sold copy. As a reader of a TREDITION CLASSICS book, you support our mission to save many of the amazing works of world literature from oblivion. See all available books at www.tredition.com.

Project Gutenberg

The content for this book has been graciously provided by Project Gutenberg. Project Gutenberg is a non-profit organization founded by Michael Hart in 1971 at the University of Illinois. The mission of Project Gutenberg is simple: To encourage the creation and distribu-tion of eBooks. Project Gutenberg is the first and largest collection of public domain eBooks.

History, Manners, and Customs of the North American Indians

Old Humphrey

Imprint

This book is part of TREDITION CLASSICS

Author: Old Humphrey
Cover design: Buchgut, Berlin – Germany

Publisher: tredition GmbH, Hamburg - Germany
ISBN: 978-3-8472-1965-1

www.tredition.com
www.tredition.de

HISTORY, MANNERS, AND CUSTOMS

OF THE

North American Indians.

BY OLD HUMPHREY.

REVISED BY THOMAS O. SUMMERS, D.D.

Nashville, Tenn.:
SOUTHERN METHODIST PUBLISHING HOUSE.
1859.

Prefatory Note.

This volume is one of a series of books from the ready and prolific pen of the late George Mogridge—better known by his *nom de plume*, "Old Humphrey." Most of his works were written for the London Religious Tract Society, and were originally issued under the auspices of that excellent institution. In revising them for our catalogue, we have found it necessary to make scarcely any alterations. A "Memoir of Old Humphrey, with Gleanings from his Portfolio"—a charming biography—accompanies our edition of his most interesting works.

Every Sunday-school and Family Library should be supplied with the entertaining and useful productions of Old Humphrey's versatile and sanctified genius.

T. O. SUMMERS.

Nashville, Tenn., Sept. 27, 1855.

PREFACE.

The present volume is in substance a reprint from a work published by the *London Religious Tract Society*, and is, we believe, chiefly compiled from the works of our enterprising countryman, Catlin. It is rendered especially attractive by the spirited and impressive pictorial illustrations of Indian life and scenery with which it abounds.

Great changes have occurred in late years, in the circumstances and prospects of the Indian tribes, and neither their number nor condition can be ascertained with much accuracy. We have endeavoured to make the present edition as correct as possible, and have omitted some parts of the original work which seemed irrelevant, or not well authenticated. We have also made such changes in the phraseology as its republication in this country requires.

INDIANS OF NORTH AMERICA [7]

CHAPTER I

It was on a wild and gusty day, that Austin and Brian Edwards were returning home from a visit to their uncle, who lived at a distance of four or five miles from their father's dwelling, [8] when the wind, which was already high, rose suddenly; and the heavens, which had for some hours been overclouded, grew darker, with every appearance of an approaching storm. Brian was for returning back; but to this Austin would by no means consent. Austin was twelve years of age, and Brian about two years younger. Their brother Basil, who was not with them, had hardly completed his sixth year.

The three brothers, though unlike in some things — for Austin was daring, Brian fearful, and Basil affectionate — very closely resembled each other in their love of books and wonderful relations. What one read, the other would read; and what one had learned, the other wished to know.

Louder and louder blew the wind, and darker grew the sky, and already had a distant flash and growling thunder announced the coming storm, when the two brothers arrived at the rocky eminence where, though the wood was above them, the river rolled nearly a hundred fathoms below. Some years before, a slip of ground had taken place at no great distance from the spot, when a mass of earth, amounting to well nigh half an acre, with the oak trees that grew upon it, slid down, all at once, towards the river. The rugged rent occasioned by the slip of earth, the great height of the road above the river, the rude rocks that here and there presented themselves, and the giant oaks of the wood frowning on the dangerous path, gave it a character at once highly picturesque and fearful. Austin, notwithstanding the [9] loud blustering of the wind, and the remonstrance of his brother to hasten on, made a momentary pause to enjoy the scene.

In a short time the two boys had approached the spot where a low, jutting rock of red sand-stone, around which the roots of a large tree were seen clinging, narrowed the path; so that there was only the space of a few feet between the base of the rock and an abrupt and fearful precipice.

Austin was looking down on the river, and Brian was holding his cap to prevent it being blown from his head, when, between the fitful blasts, a loud voice, or rather a cry, was heard. "Stop, boys, stop! come not a foot farther on peril of your lives!" Austin and Brian stood still, neither of them knowing whence came the cry, nor what was the danger that threatened them; they were, however, soon sensible of the latter, for the rushing winds swept through the wood with a louder roar, and, all at once, part of the red sand-stone rock gave way with the giant oak whose roots were wrapped round it, when the massy ruin, with a fearful crash, fell headlong across the path, and right over the precipice. Brian trembled with affright, and Austin turned pale. In another minute an active man, somewhat in years, was seen making his way over such parts of the fallen rock as had lodged on the precipice. It was he who had given the two brothers such timely notice of their danger, and thereby saved their lives.

Austin was about to thank him, but hardly had he began to speak, when the stranger stopped [10] him. "Thank God, my young friends," said he with much emotion, "and not me; for we are all in his hands. It is his goodness that has preserved you." In a little time the stranger had led Austin and Brian, talking kindly to them all the way, to his comfortable home, which was at no great distance from the bottom of the wood.

Scarcely had they seated themselves, when the storm came on in full fury. As flash after flash seemed to rend the dark clouds, the rain came down like a deluge, and the two boys were thankful to find themselves in so comfortable a shelter. Brian's attention was all taken up with the storm while Austin was surprised to see the room all hung round with lances, bows and arrows, quivers, tomahawks, and other weapons of Indian warfare together with pouches, girdles, and garments of great beauty, such as he had never before seen. A sight so unexpected both astonished and pleased him, and made a deep impression on his mind.

It was some time before the storm had spent its rage, so that the two brothers had some pleasant conversation with the stranger, who talked to them cheerfully. He did not, however, fail to dwell much on the goodness of God in their preservation; nor did he omit to urge on them to read, on their return home, the first two verses of the forty-sixth Psalm, which he said might dispose them to look upwards with thankfulness and confidence. Austin and Brian left the stranger, truly grateful for the kindness which had been shown them; and the former felt determined [11] it should not be his fault, if he did not, before long, make another visit to the place.

When the boys arrived at home, they related, in glowing colours, and with breathless haste, the adventure which had befallen them. Brian dwelt on the black clouds, the vivid lightning, and the rolling thunder; while Austin described, with startling effect, the sudden cry which had arrested their steps near the narrow path, and the dreadful crash of the red sand-stone rock, when it broke over the precipice, with the big oak-tree that grew above it. "Had we not been stopped by the cry," said he, "we must in another minute have been dashed to pieces." He then, after recounting how kind the stranger had been to them, entered on the subject of the Indian weapons.

Though the stranger who had rendered the boys so important a service was dressed like a common farmer, there was that in his manner so superior to the station he occupied, that Austin, being ardent and somewhat romantic in his notions, and wrought upon by the Indian weapons and dresses he had seen, thought he must be some important person in disguise. This belief he intimated with considerable confidence, and assigned several good reasons in support of his opinion.

Brian reminded Austin of the two verses they were to read; and, when the Bible was produced, he read aloud, "God is our refuge and strength, a very present help in trouble. Therefore will not we fear, though the earth be removed, and [12] though the mountains be carried into the midst of the sea."

"Ah," said Austin, "we had, indeed, a narrow escape; for if the mountains were not carried into the sea, the rock fell almost into the river."

On the morrow, Mr. Edwards was early on his way, to offer his best thanks, with those of Mrs. Edwards, to the stranger who had saved the lives of his children. He met him at the door, and in an interview of half an hour Mr. Edwards learned that the stranger was the son of a fur trader; and that, after the death of his father, he had spent several years among the Indian tribes, resting in their wigwams, hunting with them, and dealing in furs; but that, having met with an injury in his dangerous calling, he had at last abandoned that mode of life. Being fond of solitude, he had resolved, having the means of following out his plans, to purchase a small estate, and a few sheep; he should then be employed in the open air, and doubted not that opportunities would occur, wherein he could make himself useful in the neighbourhood. There was, also, another motive that much influenced him in his plans. His mind had for some time been deeply impressed with divine things, and he yearned for that privacy and repose, which, while it would not prevent him from attending on God's worship, would allow him freely to meditate on His holy word, which for some time had been the delight of his heart.

He told Mr. Edwards, that he had lived there for some months, and that, on entering the wood [13] the day before, close by the narrow path, he perceived by the swaying of the oak tree and moving of the sand-stone rock, that there was every probability of their falling: this had induced him to give that timely warning which had been the means, by the blessing of God, of preserving the young lads from their danger.

Mr. Edwards perceived, by his conversation and manners, that he was of respectable character; and some letters both from missionaries and ministers, addressed to the stranger, spoke loudly in favour of his piety. After offering him his best thanks, in a warm-hearted manner, and expressing freely the pleasure it would give him, if he could in any way act a neighbourly part in adding to his comfort, Mr. Edwards inquired if his children might be permitted to call at the house, to inspect the many curiosities that were there. This being readily assented to, Mr. Edwards took his departure with a very favourable impression of his new neighbour, with whom he had so unexpectedly been made acquainted.

Austin and Brian were, with some impatience, awaiting their father's return, and when they knew that the stranger who had saved their lives had actually passed years among the Indians, on the prairies and in the woods: that he had slept in their wigwams; hunted beavers, bears, and buffaloes with them; shared in their games; heard their wild war-whoop, and witnessed their battles, their delight was unbounded. Austin took large credit for his penetration in discovering that their new friend was not a common shepherd, [14] and signified his intention of becoming thoroughly informed of all the manners and customs of the North American Indians.

Nothing could have been more agreeable to the young people than this unlooked-for addition to their enjoyment. They had heard of the Esquimaux, of Negroes, Malays, New Zealanders, Chinese, Turks, and Tartars; but very little of the North American Indians. It was generally agreed, as leave had been given them to call at the stranger's, that the sooner they did it the better. Little Basil was to be of the party; and it would be a difficult thing to decide which of the three brothers looked forward to the proposed interview with the greatest pleasure.

Austin, Brian, and Basil, had at different times found abundant amusement in reading of parrots, humming birds, and cocoa nuts; lions, tigers, leopards, elephants, and the horned rhinoceros; monkeys, raccoons, opossums, and sloths; mosquitoes, lizards, snakes, and scaly crocodiles; but these were nothing in their estimation, compared with an account of Indians, bears, and buffaloes, from the mouth of one who had actually lived among them.

Indian Scenery.

CHAPTER II. [15]

Austin Edwards was too ardent in his pursuits not to make the intended visit to the cottage near the wood the continued theme of his conversation with his brothers through the remainder of the day; and, when he retired to rest, in his dreams he was either wandering through the forest defenceless, having lost his tomahawk, or flying over the prairie on the back of a buffalo, amid the yelling of a thousand Indians.

The sun was bright in the skies when the three brothers set out on their anticipated excursion. Austin was loud in praise of their kind preserver, but he could not at all understand how any one, who had been a hunter of bears and buffaloes, [16] could quietly settle down to lead the life of a farmer; for his part, he would have remained a hunter for ever. Brian thought the hunter had acted a wise part in coming away from so many dangers; and little Basil, not being quite able to decide which of his two brothers was right, remained silent.

As the two elder brothers wished to show Basil the place where they stood when the oak tree and the red sand-stone rock fell over the precipice with a crash; and as Basil was equally desirous to visit the spot, they went up to it. Austin helped his little brother over the broken fragments which still lay scattered over the narrow path. It was a sight that would have impressed the mind of any one; and Brian looked up with awe to the remaining part of the rifted rock, above which the fallen oak tree had stood. Austin was very eloquent in his description of the sudden voice of the stranger, of the roaring wind as it rushed through the wood, and of the crashing tree and falling rock. Basil showed great astonishment; and they all descended from the commanding height, full of the fearful adventure of the preceding day.

When they were come within sight of the wood, Brian cried out that he could see the shepherd's cottage; but Austin told him that he ought not to call the cottager a shepherd, but a hunter. It was true that he had a flock of sheep, but he kept them more to employ his time than to get a living by them. For many years he had lived among the Indians, and hunted buffaloes with them; he was, [17] therefore, to all intents and purposes, a buffalo hunter, and ought

not to be called a shepherd. This important point being settled—
Brian and Basil having agreed to call him, in future, a hunter, and
not a shepherd—they walked on hastily to the cottage.

In five minutes after, the hunter was showing and explaining to
his delighted young visitors the Indian curiosities which hung
around the walls of his cottage, together with others which he kept
with greater care. These latter were principally calumets, or peace-
pipes; mocassins, or Indian shoes; war-eagle dresses, mantles, neck-
laces, shields, belts, pouches and war-clubs of superior workman-
ship. There was also an Indian cradle, and several rattles and musical instruments: these altogether afforded the young people wondrous entertainment. Austin wanted to know how the Indians used
their war-clubs; Brian inquired how they smoked the peace-pipe;
and little Basil was quite as anxious in his questions about a rattle,
which he had taken up and was shaking to and fro. To all these
inquiries the hunter gave satisfactory replies, with a promise to
enter afterwards on a more full explanation.

In addition to these curiosities, the young people were shown a
few specimens of different kinds of furs: as those of the beaver,
ermine, sable, martin, fiery fox, black fox, silver fox, and squirrel.
Austin wished to know all at once, where, and in what way these
fur animals were caught; and, with this end in view, he contrived to
get the hunter into conversation on the subject. [18] "I suppose,"
said he, "that you know all about beavers, and martins, and foxes,
and squirrels."

Hunter. I ought to know something about them, having been in
my time somewhat of a *Voyageur*, a *Coureur des bois*, a *Trapper*, and a
Freeman; but you will hardly understand these terms without some
little explanation.

Austin. What is a Coureur des bois?

Brian. What is a Voyageur?

Basil. I want to know what a Trapper is.

Hunter. Perhaps it will be better if I give you a short account of
the way in which the furs of different animals are obtained, and
then I can explain the terms, Voyageur, Coureur des bois, Trapper,

and Freeman, as well as a few other things which you may like to
know.

Brian. Yes, that will be the best way.

Austin. Please not to let it be a short account, but a long one.
Begin at the very beginning, and go on to the very end.

Hunter. Well, we shall see. It has pleased God, as we read in the
first chapter of the book of Genesis, to give man "dominion over the
fish of the sea, and over the fowl of the air, and over the cattle, and
over all the earth, and over every creeping thing that creepeth upon
the earth." The meaning of which is, no doubt, not that he may cruelly abuse them, but that he may use them for his wants and comforts, or destroy them when they annoy and injure him. The skins of
animals have been used as clothing for thousands of years; and furs
have become so general in dresses and ornaments, that, to obtain
them, a regular trade [19] has long been carried on. In this traffic,
the uncivilized inhabitants of cold countries exchange their furs for
useful articles and comforts and luxuries, which are only to be obtained from warmer climes and civilized people.

Austin. And where do furs come from?

Hunter. Furs are usually obtained in cold countries. The ermine
and the sable are procured in the northern parts of Europe and Asia;
but most of the furs in use come from the northern region of our
own country.

If you look at the map of North America, you will find that between the Atlantic and the Pacific Oceans the space is, in its greatest
breath, more than three thousand miles; and, from north to south,
the country stretches out, to say the least of it, a thousand miles still
further. The principal rivers of North America are the Mackenzie,
Missouri, Mississippi, Ohio, and St. Lawrence. The Mississippi is
between three and four thousand miles long. Our country abounds
with lakes, too: Ontario and Winipeg are each near two hundred
miles long; Lakes Huron and Erie are between two and three hundred; Michigan is four hundred, and Lake Superior nearly five
hundred miles long.

Brian. What a length for a lake! nearly five hundred miles! Why, it
is more like a sea than a lake.

Hunter. Well, over a great part of the space that I have mentioned, furry animals abound; and different fur companies send those in their employ to boat up the river, to sail through the lakes, to [20] hunt wild animals, to trap beavers, and to trade with the various Indian tribes which are scattered throughout this extensive territory.

Austin. Oh! how I should like to hunt and to trade with the Indians!

Hunter. Better think the matter over a little before you set off on such an expedition. Are you ready to sail by ship, steam-boat, and canoe, to ride on horseback, or to trudge on foot, as the case may require; to swim across brooks and rivers; to wade through bogs, and swamps, and quagmires; to live for weeks on flesh, without bread or salt to it; to lie on the cold ground; to cook your own food; and to mend your own jacket and mocassins? Are you ready to endure hunger and thirst, heat and cold, rain and solitude? Have you patience to bear the stings of tormenting mosquitoes; and courage to defend your life against the grizzly bear, the buffalo, and the tomahawk of the red man, should he turn out to be an enemy?

Brian. No, no, Austin. You must not think of running into such dangers.

Hunter. I will now give you a short account of the fur trade. About two hundred years ago, or more, the French made a settlement in Canada, and they soon found such advantage in obtaining the furry skins of the various animals wandering in the woods and plains around them, that, after taking all they could themselves, they began to trade with the Indians, the original inhabitants of the country, who brought from great distances skins of various kinds. In a rude camp, formed [21] of the bark of trees, these red men assembled, seated themselves in half circles, smoked their pipes, made speeches, gave and received presents, and traded with the French people for their skins. The articles given in exchange to the Indian hunters, were knives, axes, arms, kettles, blankets, and cloth: the brighter the colour of the cloth, the better the Indians were pleased.

Austin. I think I can see them now.

Basil. Did they smoke such pipes as we have been looking at?

Hunter. Yes; for almost all the pipes used by the red men are made of red stone, dug out of the same quarry, called pipe-stone quarry; about which I will tell you some other time. One bad part of this trading system was, that the French gave the Indians but a small part of the value of their skins; and besides this they charged their own articles extravagantly high; and a still worse feature in the case was, that they supplied the Indians with spirituous liquors, and thus brought upon them all the evils and horrors of intemperance.

This system of obtaining furs was carried on for many years, when another practice sprang up. Such white men as had accompanied the Indians in hunting, and made themselves acquainted with the country, would paddle up the rivers in canoes, with a few arms and provisions, and hunt for themselves. They were absent sometimes for as much as a year, or a year and a half, and then returned with their canoes laden with rich furs. These white men were what I called *Coureurs des bois*, rangers of the woods. [22]

Austin. Ah! I should like to be a coureur des bois.

Hunter. Some of these coureurs des bois became very lawless and depraved in their habits, so that the French government enacted a law whereby no one, on pain of death, could trade in the interior of the country with the Indians, without a license. Military posts were also established, to protect the trade. In process of time, too, fur companies were established; and men, called *Voyageurs,* or canoe men, were employed, expressly to attend to the canoes carrying supplies up the rivers, or bringing back cargoes of furs.

Basil. Now we know what a *Voyageur* is.

Hunter. You would hardly know me, were you to see me dressed as a voyageur. Just think: I should have on a striped cotton shirt, cloth trousers, a loose coat made of a blanket, with perhaps leathern leggins, and deer-skin mocassins; and then I must not forget my coloured worsted belt, my knife and tobacco pouch.

Austin. What a figure you would cut! And yet, I dare say, such a dress is best for a voyageur.

Hunter. Most of the Canadian voyageurs were good-humoured, light-hearted men, who always sang a lively strain as they dipped their oars into the waters of the lake or rolling river; but steam-boats are now introduced, so that the voyageurs are but few.

Basil. What a pity! I like those voyageurs.

Hunter. The voyageurs, who were out for a long period, and navigated the interior of the [23] country, were called *North-men*, or *Winterers*, while the others had the name of *Goers and Comers*. Any part of a river where they could not row a laden canoe, on account of the rapid stream, they called a *Décharge*; and there the goods were taken from the boats, and carried on their shoulders, while others towed the canoes up the stream: but a fall of water, where they were obliged not only to carry the goods, but also to drag the canoes on land up to the higher level, they called a *Portage*.

Austin. We shall not forget the North-men, and Comers and Go-ers, nor the Décharges and Portages.

Basil. You have not told us what a Trapper is.

Hunter. A *Trapper* is a beaver hunter. Those who hunt beavers and other animals, for any of the fur companies, are called Trappers; but such as hunt for themselves take the name of *Freemen*.

Austin. Yes, I shall remember. Please to tell us how they hunt the beavers.

Hunter. Beavers build themselves houses on the banks of creeks or small rivers, with mud, sticks, and stones, and afterwards cover them over with a coat of mud, which becomes very hard. These houses are five or six feet thick at the top; and in one house four old beavers, and six or eight young ones, often live together. But, besides their houses, the beavers take care to have a number of holes in the banks, under water, called *washes*, into which they can run for shelter, should their houses be attacked. It is the business of the trappers to find out all these washes, [24] or holes; and this they do in winter, by knocking against the ice, and judging by the sound whether it is a hole. Over every hole they cut out a piece of ice, big enough to get at the beaver. No sooner is the beaver-house attacked, than the animals run into their holes, the entrances of which are directly blocked up with stakes. The trappers then either take them through the holes with their hands, or haul them out with hooks fastened to the end of a pole or stick.

Austin. But why is a beaver hunter called a trapper? I cannot understand that.

Hunter. Because beavers are caught in great numbers in steel traps, which are set and baited on purpose for them.

Brian. Why do they not catch them in the summer?

Hunter. The fur of the beaver is in its prime in the winter; in the summer, it is of inferior quality. [25]

Austin. Do the trappers catch many beavers? I should think there could not be very many of them.

Hunter. In one year, the Hudson's Bay Company alone sold as many as sixty thousand beaver-skins; and it is not a very easy matter to take them, I can assure you.

Austin. Sixty thousand! I did not think there were so many beavers in the world.

Hunter. I will tell you an anecdote, by which you will see that hunters and trappers have need to be men of courage and activity.

A trapper, of the name of Cannon, had just had the good fortune to kill a buffalo; and, as he was at a considerable distance from his camp, he cut out the tongue and some of the choice bits, made them into a parcel, and slinging them on his shoulders by a strap passed round his forehead, as the voyageurs carry packages of goods, set out on his way to the camp. In passing through a narrow ravine, he heard a noise behind him, and looking round, beheld, to his dismay, a grizzly bear in full pursuit, apparently attracted by the scent of the meat. Cannon had heard so much of the strength and ferocity of this fierce animal, that he never attempted to fire, but slipping the strap from his forehead, let go the buffalo meat, and ran for his life. The bear did not stop to regale himself with the game, but kept on after the hunter. He had nearly overtaken him, when Cannon reached a tree, and throwing down his rifle, climbed up into it. The next instant Bruin was at the foot of the tree, but as this species of [26] bear does not climb, he contented himself with turning the chase into a blockade. Night came on. In the darkness, Cannon could not perceive whether or not the enemy maintained his station; but his fears pictured him rigorously mounting guard. He passed the night, therefore, in the tree, a prey to dismal fancies. In the morning the bear was gone. Cannon warily descended the tree, picked up his gun, and made the best of his way back to the camp, without venturing to look after his buffalo-meat.

Austin. Then the grizzly bear did not hurt him, after all.

Brian. I would not go among those grizzly bears for all in the world.

Austin. Do the hunters take deer as well as other animals?

Hunter. Deer, though their skins are not so valuable as many furs, are very useful to hunters and trappers; for they not only add to their stock of peltries, but also supply them with food. When skins have been tanned on the inside, they are called *furs*; but, before they are tanned, they are called *peltries*. Deer are trapped much in the same way as buffaloes are. A large circle is enclosed with twisted trees and brushwood, with a very narrow opening, in the neighbourhood of a well-frequented deer path. The inside of the circle is crowded with small hedges, in the openings of which are set snares of twisted thongs, made fast at one end to a neighbouring tree. Two lines of small trees are set up, branching off outwardly from the narrow entrance of the [27] circle; so that the further the lines of trees extend from the circle, the wider is the space between them. As soon as the deer are seen moving in the direction of the circle, the hunters get behind them, and urge them on by loud shouts. The deer, mistaking the lines of trees set up for enemies, fly straight forward, till they enter the snare prepared for them. The circle is then surrounded, to prevent their quitting it, while some of the hunters go into it, blocking up the entrance, and kill the deer with their bows and arrows, and their spears.

Basil. I am sorry for the poor deer.

Brian. And so am I, Basil.

Hunter. Hunters are often obliged to leave food in particular places, in case they should be destitute on their return that way. They sometimes, too, leave property behind them, and for this purpose they form a *cache.*

Austin. What is a *cache?*

Hunter. A *cache* is a hole, or place of concealment; and when any thing is put in it, great care is required to conceal it from enemies, and indeed from wild animals, such as wolves and bears.

Austin. Well! but if they dig a deep hole, and put the things in it, how could anybody find it? A wolf and a bear would never find it out.

Hunter. Perhaps not; unless they should smell it.

Austin. Ay! I forgot that. I must understand a little more of my business before I set up for a hunter, or a trapper; but please to tell us all about a cache. [28]

Hunter. A cache is usually dug near a stream, that the earth taken out of the hole may be thrown into the running water, otherwise it would tell tales. Then the hunters spread blankets, or what clothes they have, over the surrounding ground, to prevent the marks of their feet being seen. When they have dug the hole they line it with dry grass, and sticks, and bark, and sometimes with a dry skin. After the things to be hidden are put in, they are covered with another dry skin, and the hole is filled up with grass, stones, and sticks, and trodden down hard, to prevent the top from sinking afterwards: the place is sprinkled with water to take away the scent; and the turf, which was first cut away, before the hole was dug, is laid down with care, just as it was before it was touched. They then take up their blankets and clothes, and leave the cache, putting a mark at some distance, that when they come again they may know where to find it.

Austin. Capital! I could make a cache now, that neither bear, nor wolf, nor Indian could find.

Brian. But if the bear did not find the cache, he might find you; and then what would become of you?

Austin. Why I would climb a tree, as Cannon did.

Hunter. Most of the furs that are taken find their way to London; but every year the animals which produce them become fewer. Besides the skins of larger animals, the furs of a great number of smaller creatures are valuable; and these, varying in their habits, require to be taken in a different [29] manner. The bison is found on the prairies, or plains; the beaver, on creeks and rivers; the badger, the fox, and the rabbit, burrow in the ground; and the bear, the deer, the mink, the martin, the raccoon, the lynx, the hare, the musk-rat, the squirrel, and ermine, are all to be found in the woods. In paddling up the rivers in canoes, and in roaming through the woods and prairies, in search of these animals, I have mingled much with Indians of different tribes; and if you can, now and then, make a call on me, you will perhaps be entertained in hearing what I can tell you about them. The Indians should be regarded by us as brothers. We ought to feel interested in their welfare here, and in their happiness hereafter. The fact that we are living on lands once the residence of these roaming tribes, and that they have been driven far into the wilderness to make room for us, should lead us not only to feel sympathy for the poor Indians, but to make decided efforts for their improvement. Our missionary societies are aiming at this great object, but far greater efforts are necessary. We have the word of God, and Christian Sabbaths, and Christian ministers, and religious ordinances, in abundance, to direct and comfort us; but they are but scantily supplied with these advantages. Let us not forget to ask in our prayers, that the Father of mercies may make known his mercy to them, opening their eyes, and influencing their hearts, so that they may become true servants of the Lord Jesus Christ.

The delight visible in the sparkling eyes of the [30] young people, as they took their leave, spoke their thanks. On their way home, they talked of nothing else but fur companies, lakes, rivers, prairies, and rocky mountains; buffaloes, wolves, bears, and beavers; and it was quite as much as Brian and Basil could do, to persuade their brother Austin from making up his mind at once to be a voyageur, a coureur des bois, or a trapper. The more they were against it, so much the more his heart seemed set upon the enterprise; and the wilder they made the buffaloes that would attack him, and the bears and wolves that would tear him to pieces, the bolder and more courageous he became. However, though on this point they could not agree, they were all unanimous in their determination to make another visit the first opportunity.

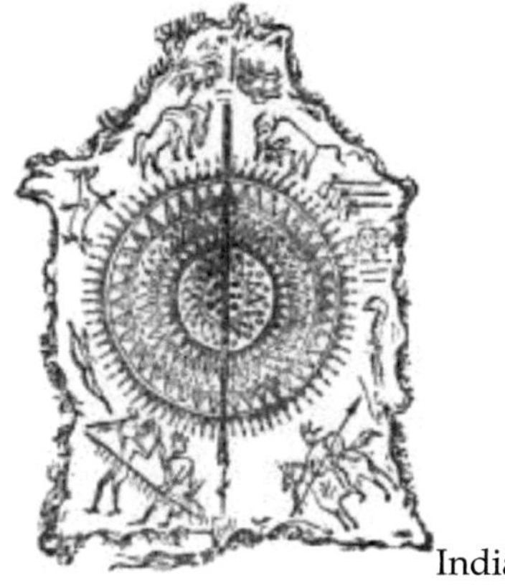

Indian Cloak.

Chiefs of different Tribes.

CHAPTER III. [31]

The next time the three brothers did not go to the red sand-stone rock, but the adventure which took place there formed a part of their conversation. They found the hunter at home, and, feeling now on very friendly and familiar terms with him, they entered at once on the subject that was nearest their hearts. "Tell us, if you please," said Austin, as soon as they were seated, "about the very beginning of the red men."

"You are asking me to do that," replied the hunter, "which is much more difficult than you suppose. To account for the existence of the original inhabitants, and of the various tribes of Indians which are now scattered throughout the whole of North America, has puzzled the [32] heads of the wisest men for ages; and, even at the present day, though travellers have endeavoured to throw light on this subject, it still remains a mystery."

Austin. But what is it that is so mysterious? What is it that wise men and travellers cannot make out?

Hunter. They cannot make out how it is, that the whole of America — taking in, as it does, some parts which are almost always covered with snow, and other parts that are as hot as the sun can make them — should be peopled with a class of human beings distinct from all others in the world — red men, who have black hair, and no beards. If you remember, it is said, in the first chapter of Genesis, "So God created man in his own image, in the image of God created he him; male and female created he them." And, in the second chapter, "And the Lord God planted a garden eastward in Eden; and there he put the man whom he had formed." Now, it is known, by the names of the rivers which are mentioned in the chapter, that the garden of Eden was in Asia; so that you see our first parents, whence the whole of mankind have sprung, dwelt in Asia.

Austin. Yes, that is quite plain.

Hunter. Well, then, you recollect, I dare say, that when the world was drowned, all mankind were destroyed, except Noah and his family in the ark.

Brian. Yes; we recollect that very well.

Hunter. And when the ark rested, it rested on Mount Ararat, which is in Asia also. If you [33] look on the map of the world, you will see that the three continents, Europe, Asia, and Africa, are united together; but America stands by itself, with an ocean rolling on each side of it, thousands of miles broad. It is easy to suppose that mankind would spread over the continents that are close together, but difficult to account for their passing over the ocean, at a time when the arts of ship-building and navigation were so little understood.

Austin. They must have gone in a ship, that is certain.

Hunter. But suppose they did, how came it about that they should be so very different from all other men? America was only discovered about four hundred years ago, and then it was well peopled with red men. Besides, there have been discovered throughout our country, monuments, ruins, and sites of ancient towns, with thousands of enclosures and fortifications. Articles, too, of pottery, sculpture, glass, and copper, have been found at times, sixty or eighty feet under the ground, and, in some instances, with forests growing over them, so that they must have been very ancient. The people who built these fortifications and towers, and possessed these articles in pottery, sculpture, glass, and copper, lived at a remote period, and must have been, to a considerable degree, cultivated. Who these people were, and how they came to America, no one knows, though many have expressed their opinions. But, even if we did know who they were, how could we account for the present race [34] of Indians in North America being barbarous, when their ancestors were so highly civilized? These are difficulties which, as I said, have puzzled the wisest heads for ages.

Austin. What do wise men and travellers say about these things?

Hunter. Some think, that as the frozen regions of Asia, in one part, are so near the frozen regions of North America—it being only about forty miles across Behring's Straits—some persons from Asia might have crossed over there, and peopled the country; or that North America might have once been joined to Asia, though it is not so now; or that, in ancient times, some persons might have drifted, or been blown there by accident, in boats or ships, across the wide ocean. Some think these people might have been Phenicians, Carthagenians, Hebrews, or Egyptians; while another class of reasoners suppose them to have been Hindoos, Chinese, Tartars, Malays, or others. It seems, however, to be God's will often to humble the pride of his creatures, by baffling their conjectures, and hedging up their opinions with difficulties. His way is in the sea, and his path in the great waters, and his footsteps are not known. He "maketh the earth empty, and maketh it waste, and turneth it upside down, and scattereth abroad the inhabitants thereof."

Austin. Well, if you cannot tell us of the Indians in former times, you can tell us of the Indians that there are, for that will be a great deal better. [35]

Brian. Yes, that it will.

Hunter. You must bear in mind, that some years have passed since I was hunting and trapping in the woods and prairies, and that many changes have taken place since then among the Indians. Some have been tomahawked by the hands of the stronger tribes; some have given up their lands to the whites, and retired to the west of the Mississippi; and thousands have been carried off by disease, which has made sad havoc among them. I must, therefore, speak of them as they were. Some of the tribes, since I left them, have been utterly destroyed; not one living creature among them being left to speak of those who have gone before them.

Austin. What a pity! They want some good doctors among them, and then diseases would not carry them off in that way.

Hunter. I will not pretend to give you an exact account of the number of the different tribes, or the particular places they now occupy; for though my information may be generally right, yet the changes which have taken place are many.

Austin. Please to tell us what you remember, and what you know; and that will quite satisfy us.

Hunter. A traveller [1] among the Indian tribes has published a book called "Letters and Notes on the Manners, Customs, and Condition of the North American Indians;" and a most interesting and entertaining account it is. If ever you can lay hold of it, it will afford you great amusement. [36] Perhaps no man who has written on the Indians has seen so much of them as he has.

[1] Mr. Catlin

Brian. Did you ever meet Catlin?

Hunter. O yes, many times; and a most agreeable companion I found him. He has lectured in most of our cities, and shown the beautiful collection of Indian dresses and curiosities collected during his visits to the remotest tribes. If you can get a sight of his book, you will soon see that he is a man of much knowledge, and possessing great courage, energy, and perseverance. I will now, then, begin my narrative; and if you can find pleasure in hearing a description of the Indians, with their villages, wigwams, war-whoops, and warriors; their manners, customs, and superstitions; their dress, ornaments, and arms; their mysteries, games, huntings, dances, war-councils, speeches, battles, and burials; with a fair sprinkling of prairie dogs, and wild horses; wolves, beavers, grizzly bears, and mad buffaloes; I will do my best to give you gratification.

Austin. These are the very things that we want to know.

Hunter. I shall not forget to tell you what the missionaries have done among the Indians; but that must be towards the latter end of my account. Let me first show you a complete table of the number and names of the tribes. It is in the Report made to Congress by the Commissioners of Indian Affairs for 1843-4. [37]

Statement showing the number of each tribe of Indians, whether natives of, or emigrants to, the country west of the Mississippi, with items of emigration and subsistence.

Names of tribes.	Number of each tribe indigenous to the country west of the Mississippi.	Number removed of each tribe wholly or partially removed.	Present western population of each tribe wholly or partially removed.	Number remaining east of each tribe.	N...
Chippewas,	—	5,779	2,298	92 [a]	

Ottowas, and Pottawatomies, and Pottawatomies of Indiana					
Creeks	—	24,594	24,594	744	
Choctaws	—	15,177	15,177	3,323	
Minatarees	2,000				
Florida Indians	—	3,824	3,824	—	212
Pagans	30,000				
Cherokees	—	25,911	25,911	1,000	
Assinaboins	—	7,000			
Swan Creek and Black River Chippewas	—	62	62	113	
Appachees	20,280				
Crees	800				
Ottowas and Chippewas, together with Chippewas of Michigan	—	—	—	7,055	
Arrapahas	2,500				
New York Indians	—	—	—	3,293	
Gros Ventres	3,300				
Chickasaws	—	4,930	4,930	80 [b]	288 [c
Eutaws	19,200				
Stockbridges and	—	180	278	320	

Munsees, and Delawares and Munsees				
Sioux	25,000			
Quapaws	476			
Iowas	470			
Kickapoos	—	588	505	
Sacs and Foxes of Mississippi	2,348 [e]			
Delawares	—	826	1,059	
Shawnees	—	1,272	887	
Sacs of Missouri	414[e]			
Weas	—	225	176	30
Osages	4,102			
Piankeshaws	—	162	98	
Kanzas	1,588			
Peorias and Kaskaskias	—	132	150	
Omahas	1,600			
Senecas from Sandusky	—	251	251	
Otoes and Missourias	931			
Senecas and Shawnees	—	211	211	
Pawnees	12,500			

Winnebagoes	—	4,500	2,183		
Camanches	19,200				
Kiowas	1,800				
Mandans	300				
Crows	4,000				
Wyandots of Ohio	—	664	—	50 [g]	664
Poncas	800				
Miamies	—	—	—	661	
Arickarees	1,200				
Menomonies	—	—	—	2,464	
Cheyenes	2,000				
Chippewas of the Lakes	—	—	—	2,564	
Blackfeet	1,300				
Caddoes	2,000				
Snakes	1,000				
Flatheads	800				
Oneidas of Green Bay	—	—	—	675	
Stockbridges of Green Bay	—	—	—	207	
Wyandots of Michigan	—	—	—	75	
Pottawatomies of Huron	—	—	—	100	

168,909   89,288   83,594   22,846   1,

NOTES.

[a] These 92 are Ottowas of Maumee.

[b] This, as far as appears from any data in the office; but, in point of fact, there are most probably no, or very few, Chickasaws remaining east.

[c] In this number is included a party, assumed to be 100, who clandestinely removed themselves; but they are withheld from the next column, because, it is not yet known what arrangement has been made for their subsistence, though instructions on that subject have been addressed to the Choctaw agent.

[d] Ten of these emigrated as far back as January, 1842; but, as the number was so small, the arrangements for their subsistence were postponed until they could be included in some larger party, such as that which subsequently arrived.

[e] These Indians do not properly belong to this column, but are so disposed of because the table is without an exactly appropriate place for them. Originally, their haunts extended east of the river, and some of their possessions on this side are among the cessions by our Indians to the Government, but their tribes have ever since been gradually moving westward.

[g] This number is conjectural, but cannot be far from the truth, as Mr. McElvaine, the sub-agent, states that but 8 or 10 families still remain. [41]

Hunter. And now, place before you a map of North America. See how it stretches out north and south from Baffin's Bay to the Gulf of Mexico, and east and west from the Atlantic to the Pacific Ocean. What a wonderful work of the Almighty is the rolling deep! "The sea is His, and he made it: and his hands formed the dry land." Here are the great Lakes Superior, Michigan, Huron, Erie, and Ontario; and here run the mighty rivers, the Mississippi, the Missouri, the Ohio, and the St. Lawrence: the Mississippi itself is between three and four thousand miles long.

Basil. What a river! Please to tell us what are all those little hills running along there, one above another, from top to bottom.

Hunter. They are the Rocky Mountains. Some regard them as a continuation of the Andes of South America; so that, if both are put together, they will make a chain of mountains little short of nine thousand miles long. North America, with its mighty lakes, rivers, and mountains, its extended valleys and prairies, its bluffs, caverns, and cataracts, and, more than all, its Indian inhabitants, beavers, buffaloes, and bisons, will afford us something to talk of for some time to come; but the moment you are tired of my account, we will stop.

Austin. We shall never be tired; no, not if you go on telling us something every time we come, for a whole year. But do tell us, how did these tribes behave to you, when you were among them? [42]

Hunter. I have not a word of complaint to make. The Indians have been represented as treacherous, dishonest, reserved, and sour in their disposition; but, instead of this, I have found them generally, though not in all cases, frank, upright, hospitable, light-hearted, and friendly. Those who have seen Indians smarting under wrongs, and deprived, by deceit and force, of their lands, hunting-grounds, and the graves of their fathers, may have found them otherwise: and no wonder; the worm that is trodden on will writhe; and man, unrestrained by Divine grace, when treated with injustice and cruelty, will turn on his oppressor.

Austin. Say what you will, I like the Indians.

Hunter. That there is much of evil among Indians is certain; much of ignorance, unrestrained passions, cruelty, and revenge: but they have been misrepresented in many things. I had better tell you the names of some of the chiefs of the tribes, or of some of the most remarkable men among them.

Austin. Yes; you cannot do better. Tell us the names of all the chiefs, and the warriors, and the conjurors, and all about them.

Hunter. The Blackfeet Indians are a very warlike people; *Stu-mick-o-súcks* was the name of their chief.

Austin. Stu-mick-o-súcks! What a name! Is there any meaning in it?

Hunter. O yes. It means, "the back fat of the buffalo;" and if you had seen him and *Peh-tó-pe-kiss,* "the ribs of the eagle," another chief [43] dressed up in their splendid mantles, buffaloes' horns, ermine tails, and scalp-locks, you would not soon have turned your eyes from them.

Brian. Who would ever be called by such a name as that? The back fat of the buffalo!

Hunter. The Camanchees are famous on horseback. There is no tribe among the Indians that can come up to them, to my mind, in the management of a horse, and the use of the lance: they are capital hunters. The name of their chief is *Eé-shah-kó-nee,* or "the bow and quiver." I hardly ever saw a larger man among the Indians than *Ta-wáh-que-nah,* the second chief in power. Ta-wáh-que-nah means "the mountain of rocks," a very fit name for a huge Indian living near the Rocky Mountains. When I saw *Kots-o-kó-ro-kó,* or "the hair of the bull's neck," (who is, if I remember right, the third chief,) he had a gun in his right hand, and his warlike shield on his left arm.

Austin. If I go among the Indians, I shall stay a long time with the Camanchees; and then I shall, perhaps, become one of the most skilful horsemen, and one of the best hunters in the world.

Brian. And suppose you get thrown off your horse, or killed in hunting buffaloes, what shall you say to it then?

Austin. Oh, very little, if I get killed; but no fear of that. I shall mind what I am about. Tell us who is the head of the Sioux?

Hunter. When I was at the upper waters of the Mississippi and Missouri rivers, *Ha-wón-je-tah,* [44] or "the one horn," was chief; but since then, being out among the buffaloes, a buffalo bull attacked and killed him.

Basil. There, Austin! If an Indian chief was killed by a buffalo, what should *you* do among them? Why they would toss you over their heads like a shuttlecock.

Hunter. *Wee-tá-ra-sha-ro,* the head chief of the Pawnee Picts, is dead now, I dare say; for he was a very old, as well as a very venerable looking man. Many a buffalo hunt with the Camanchees had he in his day, and many a time did he go forth with them in their war-parties. He had a celebrated brave of the name of *Ah'-sho-cole,* or "rotten foot," and another called *Ah'-re-kah-na-có-chee,* "the mad elk." Indians give the name of *brave* to a warrior who has distinguished himself by feats of valour, such as admit him to their rank.

Brian. I wonder that they should choose such long names. It must be a hard matter to remember them.

Hunter. There were many famous men among the Sacs. *Kee-o-kuk* was the chief. Kee-o-kuk means "the running fox." One of his boldest braves was *Má-ka-tai-me-she-kiá-kiák,* "the black hawk." The history of this renowned warrior is very curious. It was taken down from his own lips, and has been published. If you should like to listen to the adventures of Black Hawk, I will relate them to you some day, when you have time to hear them, as well as those of young Nik-ka-no-chee, a Seminole. [45]

Austin. We will not forget to remind you of your promise. It will be capital to listen to these histories.

Hunter. When I saw *Wa-sáw-me-saw,* or "the roaring thunder," the youngest son of Black Hawk, he was in captivity. *Náh-se-ús-kuk,* "the whirling thunder," his eldest son, was a fine looking man, beautifully formed, with a spirit like that of a lion. There was a war called The Black Hawk war, and Black Hawk was the leader and conductor of it; and one of his most famous warriors was *Wah-pe-kée-suck,* or "white cloud;" he was, however, as often called The Prophet as the White Cloud. *Pam-a-hó,* "the swimmer;" *Wah-pa-ko-lás-kak,* "the track of the bear;" and *Pash-ce-pa-hó,* "the little stabbing chief;" were, I think, all three of them warriors of Black Hawk.

Basil. The Little Stabbing Chief! He must be a very dangerous fellow to go near, if we may judge by his name: keep away from him, Austin, if you go to the Sacs.

Austin. Oh! he would never think of stabbing me. I should behave well to all the tribes, and then I dare say they would all of them behave well to me. You have not said any thing of the Crow Indians.

Hunter. I forget who was at the head of the Crows, though I well remember several of the warriors among them. They were tall, well-proportioned, and dressed with a great deal of taste and care. *Pa-ris-ka-roó-pa,* called "the two crows," had a head of hair that swept the ground after him as he walked along. [46]

Austin. What do you think of that, Basil? No doubt the Crows are fine fellows. Please to mention two or three more.

Hunter. Let me see; there was *Eé-heé-a-duck-chée-a,* or "he who binds his hair before;" and *Hó-ra-to-ah,* "a warrior;" and *Chah-ee-chópes,* "the four wolves;" the hair of these was as long as that of Pa-ris-ka-roó-pa. Though they were very tall, Eé-heé-a-duck-chée-a being at least six feet high, the hair of each of them reached and rested on the ground.

Austin. When I go among the Indians, the Crows shall not be forgotten by me. I shall have plenty to tell you of, Brian, when I come back.

Brian. Yes, if you ever do come back; but what with the sea, and the rivers, and the swamps, and the bears, and the buffaloes, you are sure to get killed. You will never tell us about the Crows, or about any thing else.

Hunter. There was one of the Crows called The Red Bear, or *Duhk-pits-o-hó-shee.*

Brian. Duhk-pitch a — Duck pits — I cannot pronounce the word — why that is worse to speak than any.

Austin. Hear me pronounce it then: *Duhk-pits-o-hoot-shee.* No; that is not quite right, but very near it.

Basil. You must not go among the Crows yet, Austin; you cannot talk well enough.

Hunter. Oh, there are much harder names among some of the tribes than those I have mentioned; for instance there is *Aú-nah-kwet-to-hau-páy-o,* "the one sitting in the clouds;" and [47] *Eh-tohk-pay-she-peé-shah,* "the black mocassin;" and *Kay-ée-qua-da-kúm-ée-gish-kum,* "he who tries the ground with his foot;" and *Mah-to-rah-rish-nee-éeh-ee-rah,* "the grizzly bear that runs without fear."

Brian. Why these names are as long as from here to yonder. Set to work, Austin! set to work! For, if there are many such names as these among the Indians, you will have enough to do without going to a buffalo hunt.

Austin. I never dreamed that there were such names as those in the world.

Basil. Ay, you will have enough of them, Austin, if you go abroad. You will never be able to learn them, do what you will. Give it up, Austin; give it up at once.

Though Brian and Basil were very hard on Austin on their way home, about the long names of the Indians, and the impossibility of his ever being able to learn them by heart, Austin defended himself stoutly. "Very likely," said he, "after all, they call these long names very short, just as we do; Nat for Nathaniel, Kit for Christopher, and Elic for Alexander."

Wigwams.

CHAPTER IV. [48]

It was not long before Austin, Brian, and Basil were again listening to the interesting accounts given by their friend, the hunter; and it would have been a difficult point to decide whether the listeners or the narrator derived most pleasure from their occupation. Austin began without delay to speak of the aborigines of North America.

"We want to know," said he, "a little more about what these people were, and when they were first found out."

Hunter. When America was first discovered, the inhabitants, though for the most part partaking of one general character, were not without variety. The greater part, as I told you, were, both in hot [49] and cold latitudes, red men with black hair, and without beards. They, perhaps, might have been divided into four parts: the Mexicans and Peruvians, who were, to a considerable extent, civilized; the Caribs, who inhabited the fertile soil and luxuriant clime of the West Indies; the Esquimaux, who were then just the same people as they are now, living in the same manner by fishing; and the Red Men, or North American Indians.

Austin. Then the Esquimaux are not Red Indians.

Hunter. No; they are more like the people who live in Lapland, and in the North of Asia; and for this reason, and because the distance across Behring's Straits is so short, it is thought they came from Asia, and are a part of the same people. The red men are, however, different; and as we agreed that I should tell you about the present race of them, perhaps I may as well proceed.

Austin. Yes. Please to tell us first of their wigwams, and their villages, and how they live.

Brian. And what they eat, and what clothes they wear.

Basil. And how they talk to one another.

Austin. Yes; and all about their spears and tomahawks.

Hunter. The wigwams of the Indians are of different kinds: some are extremely simple, being formed of high sticks or poles, covered with turf or the bark of trees; while others are very handsome. The

Sioux, the Blackfeet, and the Crows, [50] form their wigwams nearly in the same manner; that is, by sewing together the skins of buffaloes, after properly dressing them, and making them into the form of a tent. This covering is then supported by poles. The tent has a hole at the top, to let out the smoke, and to let in the light.

Austin. Ay, that is a better way of making a wigwam than covering over sticks with turf.

Hunter. The wigwams, or lodges, of the Mandans are round. A circular foundation is dug about two feet deep; timbers six feet high are set up all around it, and on these are placed other long timbers, slanting inwards, and fastened together in the middle, like a tent, leaving space for light and for the smoke to pass. This tent-like roof is supported by beams and upright posts, and it is covered over outwardly by willow boughs and a thick coating of earth; then comes the last covering of hard tough clay. The sun bakes this, and long use makes it solid. The outside of a Mandan lodge is almost as useful as the inside; for there the people sit, stand, walk, and take the air. These lodges are forty, fifty, or sixty feet wide.

Brian. The Mandan wigwam is the best of all.

Hunter. Wigwams, like those of the Mandans, which are always in the same place, and are not intended to be removed, are more substantial than such as may be erected and taken down at pleasure. Some of the wigwams of the Crow Indians, covered as they are with skins dressed almost white, and ornamented with paint, porcupine quills and scalp-locks, are very beautiful.

Austin. Yes; they must look even better than [51] the Mandan lodges, and they can be taken down and carried away.

Hunter. It would surprise you to witness the manner in which an encampment of Crows or Sioux strike their tents or wigwams. I have seen several hundred lodges all standing; in two or three minutes after, all were flat upon the prairie.

Austin. Why, it must be like magic.

Hunter. The time has been fixed, preparations made, the signal given, and all at once the poles and skin coverings have been taken down.

Brian. How do they carry the wigwams away with them?

Hunter. The poles are dragged along by horses and by dogs; the smaller ends being fastened over their shoulders, while on the larger ends, dragging along the ground, are placed the coverings, rolled up together. The dogs pull along two poles, each with a load, while the horses are taxed according to their strength. Hundreds of horses and dogs, thus dragging their burdens, may be seen slowly moving over the prairie with attendant Indians on horseback, and women and girls on foot heavily laden.

Brian. What a sight! and to what length they must stretch out; such a number of them!

Hunter. Some of their villages are large, and fortified with two rows of high poles round them. A Pawnee Pict village on the Red River, with its five or six hundred beehive-like wigwams of poles, thatched with prairie grass, much pleased me. Round the village there were fields of maize, melons and pumpkins growing. [52]

The Indians hunt, fish, and some of them raise corn for food; but the flesh of the buffalo is what they most depend upon.

Austin. How do the Indians cook their food?

Hunter. They broil or roast meat and fish, by laying it on the fire, or on sticks raised above the fire. They boil meat, also, making of it a sort of soup. I have often seated myself, squatting down on a robe spread for me, to a fine joint of buffalo ribs, admirably roasted; with, perhaps, a pudding-like paste of the prairie turnip, flavoured with buffalo berries.

Austin. That is a great deal like an English dinner — roast beef and a pudding.

Hunter. The Indians eat a great deal of green corn, pemican, and marrow fat. The pemican is buffalo meat, dried hard, and pounded in a wooden mortar. Marrow fat is what is boiled out of buffalo bones; it is usually kept in bladders. They eat, also, the flesh of the deer and other animals: that of the dog is reserved for feasts and especial occasions. They have, also, beans and peas, peaches, melons and strawberries, pears, pumpkins, chinkapins, walnuts and chestnuts. These things they can get when settled in their villages;

but when wandering, or on their war parties, they take up with what they can find. They never eat salt with their food.

Basil. And what kind of clothes do they wear?

Hunter. Principally skins, unless they trade with the whites, in which case they buy clothes of different kinds. Some wear long hair, some cut their hair off and shave the head. Some [53] dress themselves with very few ornaments, but others have very many. Shall I describe to you the full dress of *Máh-to-tóh-pa,* "the four bears."

Austin. Oh, yes; every thing belonging to him.

Hunter. You must imagine, then, that he is standing up before you, while I describe him, and that he is not a little proud of his costly attire.

Austin. I fancy that I can see him now.

Hunter. His robe was the soft skin of a young buffalo bull. On one side was the fur; on the other, were pictured the victories he had won. His shirt, or tunic, was made of the skins of mountain sheep, ornamented with porcupine quills and paintings of his battles. From the edge of his shoulder-band hung the long black locks that he had taken with his own hand from his enemies. His head-dress was of war-eagle quills, falling down his back to his very feet; on the top of his head stood a pair of buffalo horns, shaven thin, and polished beautifully.

Brian. What a figure he must have made!

Hunter. His leggings were tight, decorated with porcupine quills and scalp-locks: they were made of the finest deer skins, and fastened to a belt round the waist. His mocassins, or shoes, were buckskin, embroidered in the richest manner; and his necklace, the skin of an otter, having on it fifty huge claws, or rather talons, of the grizzly bear.

Austin. What a desperate fellow! Bold as a lion, I will be bound for it. Had he no weapons about him?

Hunter. Oh, yes! He held in his left hand a [54] two-edged spear of polished steel, with a shaft of tough ash, and ornamented with tufts of war-eagle quills. His bow, beautifully white, was formed of bone, strengthened with the sinews of deer, drawn tight over the back of it; the bow-string was a three-fold twist of sinews. Seldom had its twang been heard, without an enemy or a buffalo falling to the earth; and rarely had that lance been urged home, without finding its way to some victim's heart.

Austin. Yes; I thought he was a bold fellow.

Hunter. He had a costly shield of the hide of a buffalo, stiffened with glue and fringed round with eagle quills and antelope hoofs; and a quiver of panther skin, well filled with deadly shafts. Some of their points were flint, and some were steel, and most of them were stained with blood. He carried a pipe, a tobacco sack, a belt, and a medicine bag; and in his right hand he held a war club like a sling, being made of a round stone wrapped up in a raw hide and fastened to a tough stick handle.

Austin. What sort of a pipe was it?

Basil. What was in his tobacco sack?

Brian. You did not say what his belt was made of.

Hunter. His pipe was made of red pipe-stone, and it had a stem of young ash, full three feet long, braided with porcupine quills in the shape of animals and men. It was also ornamented with the beaks of woodpeckers, and hairs from the tail of the white buffalo. One thing I ought not to omit; on the lower half of the pipe, which [55] was painted red, were notched the snows, or years of his life. By this simple record of their lives, the red men of the forest and the prairie may be led to something like reflection.

Basil. What was in his tobacco sack?

Hunter. His flint and steel, for striking a light, and his tobacco, which was nothing more than the bark of the red willow. His medicine bag was beaver skin, adorned with ermine and hawks' bills; and his belt, in which he carried his tomahawk and scalping-knife, was formed of tough buckskin, firmly fastened round his loins.

Austin. Please to tell us about the scalping knife. It must be a fearful instrument.

Hunter. All instruments of cruelty, vengeance and destruction are fearful, whether in savage or civilized life. What are we, that wrath and revenge and covetousness should be fostered in our hearts!

What is man, that he should shed the blood of his brother! Before the Indians had dealing with the whites, they made their own weapons: their bows were strung with the sinews of deer; their arrows were headed with flint; their knives were sharpened bone; their war-clubs were formed of wood, cut into different shapes, and armed with sharp stones; and their tomahawks, or hatchets, were of the same materials: but now, many of their weapons, such as hatchets, spear-heads, and knives, are made of iron, being procured from the whites, in exchange for the skins they obtain in the chase. A scalping-knife is oftentimes no more than a rudely formed butcher's [56] knife, with one edge, and the Indians wear them in beautiful scabbards under their belts.

Austin. How does an Indian scalp his enemy?

Hunter. The hair on the crown of the head is seized with the left hand; the knife makes a circle round it through the skin, and then the hair and skin together, sometimes with the hand, and sometimes with the teeth, are forcibly torn off! The scalp may be, perhaps, as broad as my hand.

Brian. Terrible! Scalping would be sure to kill a man, I suppose.

Hunter. Not always. Scalps are war trophies, and are generally regarded as proofs of the death of an enemy; but an Indian, inflamed with hatred and rage, and excited by victory, will not always wait till his foe has expired before he scalps him. The hair, as well as the scalp, of a fallen foe is carried off by the victorious Indian, and with it his clothes are afterwards ornamented. It is said, that, during the old French war, an Indian slew a Frenchman who wore a wig. The warrior stooped down, and seized the hair for the purpose of securing the scalp. To his great astonishment, the wig came off, leaving the head bare. The Indian held it up, and examining it with great wonder, exclaimed, in broken English, "Dat one big lie."

Brian. How the Indian would stare!

Basil. He had never seen a wig before, I dare say.

Hunter. The arms of Indians, offensive and defensive, are, for the most part, those which I have mentioned — the club, the tomahawk, the bow [57] and arrow, the spear, the shield and the scalping-knife. But the use of fire-arms is gradually extending among them. Some of their clubs are merely massy pieces of hard, heavy wood, nicely fitted to the hand, with, perhaps, a piece of hard bone stuck in the head part; others are curiously carved into fanciful and uncouth shapes; while, occasionally, may be seen a frightful war-club, knobbed all over with brass nails, with a steel blade at the end of it, a span long.

Austin. What a terrible weapon, when wielded by a savage!

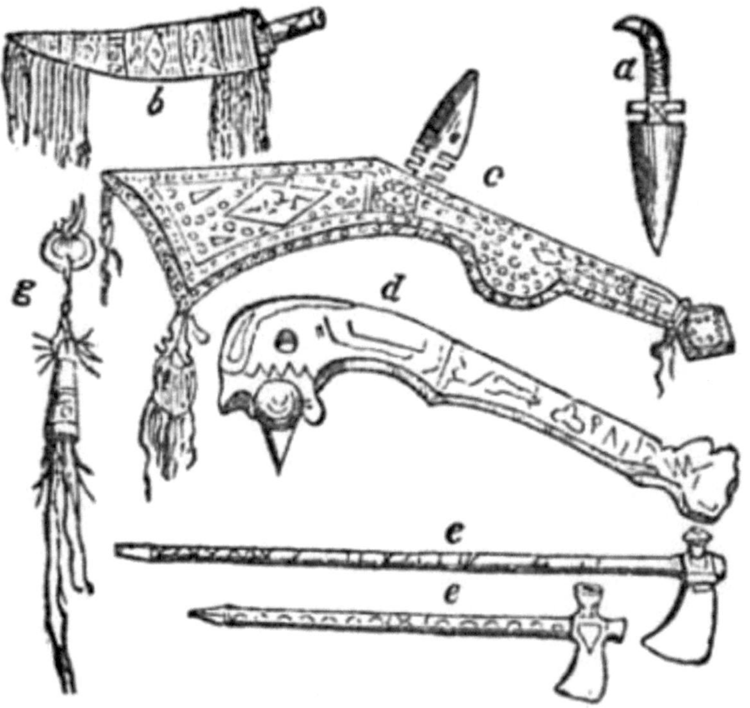

a, scalping-knife. *b*, ditto, in sheath. *c*, *d*, war-clubs. *e*, *e*, tomahawks. *g*, whip.

Brian. I would not go among the Indians, with their clubs and tomahawks, for a thousand dollars.

Basil. Nor would I: they would be sure to kill me.

Hunter. The tomahawk is often carved in a strange manner; and some of the bows and arrows [58] are admirable. The bow formed of bone and strong sinews is a deadly weapon; and some Indians have boasted of having sent an arrow from its strings right through the body of a buffalo.

Austin. What a strong arm that Indian must have had! Through a buffalo's body!

Hunter. The quiver is made of the skin of the panther, or the otter; and some of the arrows it contains are usually poisoned.

Brian. Why, then, an arrow is sure to kill a person, if it hits him.

Hunter. It is not likely that an enemy, badly wounded with a poisoned arrow, will survive; for the head is set on loosely, in order that, when the arrow is withdrawn, the poisoned barb may remain in the wound. How opposed are these cruel stratagems of war to the precepts of the gospel of peace, which are "Love your enemies, bless them that curse you, do good to them that hate you, and pray for them which despitefully use you, and persecute you!"

Basil. What will you do, Austin, if you go among the Indians, and they shoot you with a poisoned arrow?

Austin. Oh, I shall carry a shield. You heard that the Indians carry shields.

Hunter. The shields of the Crows and Blackfeet are made of the thick skin of the buffalo's neck: they are made as hard as possible, by smoking them, and by putting glue upon them obtained from the hoofs of animals; so that they will not only turn aside an arrow, but even a musket ball, if they are held a little obliquely. [59]

Austin. There, Basil! You see that I shall be safe, after all; for I shall carry a large shield, and the very hardest I can get anywhere.

Hunter. Their spears have long, slender handles, with steel heads: the handles are a dozen feet long, or more, and very skilful are they in the use of them; and yet, such is the dread of the Indian when opposed to a white man, that, in spite of his war horse and his eagle plumes, his bow and well-filled quiver, his long lance, tomahawk and scalping-knife, his self-possession forsakes him. He has heard, if not seen, what the white man has done; and he thinks there is no standing before him. If he can surprise him, he will; but, generally, the red man fears to grapple with a pale face in the strife of war, for he considers him clothed with an unknown power.

Austin. I should have thought that an Indian would be more than a match for a white man.

Hunter. So long as he can crawl in the grass or brushwood, and steal silently upon him by surprise, or send a shaft from his bow from behind a tree, or a bullet from his rifle from the brow of a bluff, he has an advantage; but, when he comes face to face with the white man, he is superstitiously afraid of him. The power of the white man, in war, is that of bravery and skill; the power of the red man consists much in stratagem and surprise. Fifty white men, armed, on an open plain, would beat off a hundred red men.

Brian. Why is it that the red men are always fighting against one another? They are all [60] brothers, and what is the use of their killing one another?

Hunter. Most of the battles, among the Indians, are brought about by the belief that they are bound to revenge an injury to their tribe. There can be no peace till revenge is taken; they are almost always retaliating one on another. Then, again, the red men have too often been tempted, bribed, and, in some cases, forced to fight for the white man.

Brian. That is very sad, though.

Hunter. It is sad; but when you say red men are brothers, are not white men brothers too? And have they not been instructed in the truths of Christianity, and the gospel of peace, which red men have not, and yet how ready they are to draw the sword! War springs from sinful passions; and until sin is subdued in the human heart, war will ever be congenial to it.

Austin. What do the Indians call the sun?

Hunter. The different tribes speak different languages, and therefore you must tell me which of them you mean.

Austin. Oh! I forgot that. Tell me what any two or three of the tribes call it.

Hunter. A Sioux calls it *wee*; a Mandan, *menahka*; a Tuscarora, *hi-day*; and a Blackfoot, *cristeque ahtose*.

Austin. The Blackfoot is the hardest to remember. I should not like to learn that language.

Brian. But you must learn it, if you go among them; or else you will not understand a word they say. [61]

Austin. Well! I shall manage it somehow or other. Perhaps some of them may know English; or we may make motions one to another. What do they call the moon?

Hunter. A Blackfoot calls it *coque ahtose*; a Sioux, *on wee*; a Riccaree, *wetah*; a Mandan, *esto menahka*; and a Tuscarora, *autsunyehaw*.

Brian. I wish you joy of the languages you have to learn, Austin, if you become a wood-ranger, or a trapper. Remember, you must learn them all; and you will have quite enough to do, I warrant you.

Austin. Oh! I shall learn a little at a time. We cannot do every thing at once. What do the red men call a buffalo?

Hunter. In Riccaree, it is *watash*; in Mandan, *ptemday*; in Tuscarora, *hohats*; in Blackfoot, *eneuh*.

Basil. What different names they give them!

Hunter. Yes. In some instances they are alike, but generally they differ. If you were to say "How do you do?" as is the custom with us; you must say among the Indians, *How ke che wa? Chee na e num? Dati youthay its?* or, *Tush hah thah mah kah hush?* according to the language in which you spoke. I hardly think these languages would suit you so well as your own.

Brian. They would never suit me; but Austin must learn every word of them.

Austin. Please to tell us how to count ten, and then we will ask you no more about languages. Let it be in the language of the Ricca-rees. [62]

Hunter. Very well. *Asco, pitco, tow wit, tchee tish, tchee hoo, tcha pis, to tcha pis, to tcha pis won, nah e ne won, nah en.* I will just add, that *weetah*, is twenty; *nahen tchee hoo*, is fifty; *nah en te tcha pis won*, is eighty; *shok tan*, is a hundred; and *sho tan tera hoo*, is a thousand.

Austin. Can the Indians write?

Hunter. Oh no; they have no use for pen and ink, excepting some of the tribes near the whites. In many of the different treaties which have been made between the white and the red man, the latter has put, instead of his name, a rough drawing of the animal or thing after which he had been called. If the Indian chief was named "War hatchet," he made a rough outline of a tomahawk. If his name was "The great buffalo" then the outline of a buffalo was his signature.

Basil. How curious!

Hunter. The *Big turtle*, the *Fish*, the *Scalp*, the *Arrow*, and the *Big canoe*, all draw the form represented by their names in the same manner. If you were to see these signatures, you would not think these Indian chiefs had ever taken lessons in drawing.

Brian. I dare say their fish, and arrows, and hatchets, and turtles, and buffaloes, are comical figures enough.

Hunter. Yes: but the hands that make these feeble scrawls are strong, when they wield the bow or the tomahawk. A white man in the Indian country, according to a story that is told, met a Shawnese riding a horse, which he recognised as his own, and claimed it as his property. [63] The Indian calmly answered: "Friend, after a little while I will call on you at your house, when we will talk this matter over." A few days afterwards, the Indian came to the white man's house, who insisted on having his horse restored to him. The other then told him: "Friend, the horse which you claim belonged to my uncle, who lately died; according to the Indian custom, I have become heir to all his property." The white man not being satisfied, and renewing his demand, the Indian immediately took a coal from the fire-place, and made two striking figures on the door of the house; the one representing the white man taking the horse, and the other himself in the act of scalping him: then he coolly asked the trembling claimant whether he could read this Indian writing. The matter was thus settled at once, and the Indian rode off.

Austin. Ay; the white man knew that he had better give up the horse than be scalped.

After the hunter had told Austin and his brothers that he should be sure to have something new to tell them on their next visit, they took their departure, having quite enough to occupy their minds till they reached home.

CHAPTER V. [64]

"Black Hawk! Black Hawk!" cried out Austin Edwards, as he came in sight of the hunter, who was just returning to his cottage as Austin and his brothers reached it. "You promised to tell us all about Black Hawk, and we are come to hear it now."

The hunter told the boys that it had been his intention to talk with them about the prairies and bluffs, and to have described the wondrous works of God in the wilderness. It appeared, however, that Austin's heart was too much set on hearing [65] the history of Black Hawk, to listen patiently to any thing else; and the hunter, perceiving this, willingly agreed to gratify him. He told them, that, in reading or hearing the history of Indian chiefs, they must not be carried away by false notions of their valour, for that it was always mingled with much cruelty. The word of God said truly, that "the dark places of the earth are full of the habitations of cruelty." [2] "With untaught Indians," continued he, "revenge is virtue; and to tomahawk an enemy, and tear away his scalp, is the noblest act he can perform in his own estimation; whereas Christians are taught, as I said before, to forgive and love their enemies. But I will now begin the history of Black Hawk."

[2] Ps. lxxiv. 20.

Austin. Suppose you tell us his history just as he would tell it himself. Speak to us as if you were Black Hawk, and we will not say a single word.

Hunter. Very well. Then, for a while, I will be Black Hawk, and what I tell you will be true, only the words will be my own, instead of those of the Indian chief. And I will speak as if I spoke to American white men.

"I am an old man, the changes of many moons and the toils of war have made me old. I have been a conqueror, and I have been conquered: many moons longer I cannot hope to live.

"I have hated the whites, but have been treated well by them when a prisoner. I wish, before I go my long journey, at the command of the Great Spirit, to the hunting grounds of my fathers in

[66] another world, to tell my history; it will then be seen why I hated the whites. Bold and proud was I once, in my native forests, but the pale faces deceived me; it was for this that I hated them.

"Would you know where I was born? I will tell you. It was at the Sac village on Rock River. This was, according to white man's reckoning, in the year 1767, so that I am fifty years old, and ten and seven.

"My father's name was Py-e-sa; the father of his father was Na-nà-ma-kee, or Thunder. I was a brave, and afterwards a chief, a leading war-chief, carrying the medicine bag. I fought against the Osages. Did I fear them? No. Did I often win the victory? I did.

"The white men of America said to the Sacs and Foxes, to the Sioux, the Chippewas, and Winnebagoes, 'Go you to the other side of the Mississippi;' and they said, 'Yes.' But I said, 'No: why should I leave the place where our wigwams stand, where we have hunted for so many moons, and where the bones of our fathers have rested? Ma-ka-tai-me-she-kia-kiak, or Black Hawk, will not go.'

"My heart told me that my great white father, the chief of America, would not do wrong; would not make me go to the other side of the river. My prophet also told me the same. I felt my arm strong, and I fought. Never did the hand of Black Hawk kill woman or child. They were warriors that Black Hawk fought with.

"Though I came down from the chief Na-nà-ma-kee, yet my people would not let me dress like [67] a chief. I did not paint myself; I did not wear feathers; but I was bold and not afraid to fight, so I became a brave.

"The Osages were our enemies, and I went with my father and many more to fight. I saw my father kill an enemy, and tear away the scalp from his head. I felt determined to do the same. I pleased my father; for, with my tomahawk and spear, I rushed on an enemy. I brought back his scalp in my hand.

"I next led on seven of our people against a hundred Osages, and killed one. After that, I led on two hundred, when we killed a hundred, and took many scalps. In a battle with the Cherokees my father was killed. I painted my face black, and prayed to the Great

Spirit, and did not fight any more for five years; all that I did was to hunt and to fish.

"The Osages had done us great wrong, so we were determined to destroy them. I set off, in the third moon, at the head of five hundred Sacs and Foxes, and one hundred Ioways. We fell upon forty lodges. I made two of their squaws prisoners, but all the rest of the people in the lodges we killed. Black Hawk killed seven men himself. In a battle with the Cherokees, I killed thirteen of their bravest with my own hand.

"One of our people killed a pale-face American, and he was put in prison; so we sent to St. Louis, to pay for the killed man, and to cover the blood. Did the pale faces do well? No, they did not; they set our man free, but when he began to run they shot him down; and they gave strong [68] drink to our four people, and told them to give up the best part of our hunting ground for a thousand dollars every twelve moons. What right had they to give our men strong drink, and then cheat them? None.

"American white faces came, with a great, big gun, to build a fort, and said it was to trade with us. They treated the Indians ill: we went against the fort. I dug a hole in the ground with my knife, so that I could hide myself with some grass. I shot with my rifle and cut the cord of their flag, so that they could not pull it up to fly in the air; and we fired the fort, but they put out the fire.

"One of our people killed a white, and was taken. He was to die, but asked leave to go and see his squaw and children. They let him go, but he ran back through the prairies next day, in time to be shot down. He did not say he would come back, and then stay; he was an Indian, and not a white man. I hunted and fished for his squaw and children when he was dead.

"Why was it that the Great Spirit did not keep the white men where he put them? Why did he let them come among my people with their fire-drink, sickness, and guns? It had been better for red men to be by themselves.

"We went to a great English brave, Colonel Dixon, at Green Bay: there were many Pottawatomies, Kickapoos, Ottowas, and Winnebagoes there. The great brave gave us pipes, tobacco, new guns, powder, and clothes. I held a talk with him in his tent; he took my hand. 'General Black Hawk,' said he, and he put a medal [69] round my neck, 'you must now hold us fast by the hand; you will have the command of all the braves to join our own braves at Detroit.' I was sorry, because I wanted to go to Mississippi. But he said, 'No; you are too brave to kill women and children: you must kill braves.'

"We had a feast, and I led away five hundred braves to join the British. Sometimes we won, and sometimes we lost. The Indians were killing the prisoners, but Black Hawk stopped them. He is a coward who kills a brave that has no arms and cannot fight. I did not like so often to be beaten in battle, and to get no plunder. I left the British, with twenty of my braves, to go home, and see after my wife and children.

"I found an old friend of mine sitting on a mat in sorrow: he had come to be alone, and to make himself little before the Great Spirit: he had fasted long, he was hardly alive; his son had been taken prisoner, and shot and stabbed to death. I put my pipe to my friend's mouth; he smoked a little. I took his hand, and said 'Black Hawk would revenge his son's death.' A storm came on; I wrapped my old friend in my blanket. The storm gave over; I made a fire. It was too late; my friend was dead. I stopped with him the remainder of the night; and then my people came, and we buried him on the peak of the bluff.

"I explained to my people the way the white men fight. Instead of stealing on each other, quietly and by surprise, to kill their enemies and save their own people, they all fight in the sunlight, like braves; not caring how many of their [70] people fall. They then feast and drink as if nothing had happened, and write on paper that they have won, whether they have won or been beaten. And they do not write truth, for they only put down a part of the people they have lost. They would do to *paddle* a canoe, but not to *steer* it. They fight like braves, but they are not fit to be chiefs, and to lead war parties.

"I found my wife well, and my children, and would have been quiet in my lodge; for, while I was away, Kee-o-kuk had been made a chief: but I had to revenge the death of the son of my old friend. I told my friend so when he was dying. Why should Black Hawk speak a lie? I took with me thirty braves, and went to Fort Madison;

but the American pale faces had gone. I was glad, but still followed them down the Mississippi. I went on their trail. I shot the chief of the party with whom we fought. We returned home, bringing two scalps. Black Hawk had done what he said.

"Many things happened. Old Wàsh-e-own, one of the Pottawatomies, was shot dead by a war chief. I gave Wàsh-e-own's relations two horses and my rifles to keep the peace. A party of soldiers built a fort at Prairie du Chien. They were friendly to us, but the British came and took the fort. We joined them; we followed the boats and shot fire-arrows, and the sails of one boat were burned, and we took it.

"We found, in the boats we had taken, barrels of whiskey: this was bad medicine. We knocked in the heads of the barrels, and emptied out [71] the bad medicine. We found bottles and packages, which we flung into the river as bad medicine too. We found guns and clothes, which I divided with my braves. The Americans built a fort; I went towards it with my braves. I had a dream, in which the Great Spirit told me to go down the bluff to a creek, and to look in a hollow tree cut down, and there I should see a snake; close by would be the enemy unarmed. I went to the creek, peeped into the tree, saw the snake, and found the enemy. One man of them was killed, after that we returned home: peace was made between the British and Americans, and we were to bury the tomahawk too.

"We went to the great American chief at St. Louis, and smoked the pipe of peace. The chief said our great American father was angry with us, and accused us of crimes. We said this was a lie; for our great father had deceived us, and forced us into a war. They were angry at what we said; but we smoked the pipe of peace again, and I first touched the goose quill; but I did not know that, in doing so, I gave away my village. Had I known it, I would never have touched the goose quill.

"The American whites built a fort on Rock Island; this made us sorry, for it was our garden, like what the white people have near their big villages. It supplied us with plums, apples and nuts, with strawberries and blackberries. Many happy days had I spent on Rock Island. A good spirit had the care of it; he lived under the rock, in a cave. He was white, and his wings were ten times bigger

[72] than swan's wings: when the white men came there, he went away.

"We had corn and beans and pumpkins and squashes. We were the possessors of the valley of the Mississippi, full seven hundred miles from the Ouisconsin to the Portage des Sioux, near the mouth of the Missouri. If another prophet had come to us in those days, and said, 'The white man will drive you from these hunting grounds, and from this village, and Rock Island, and not let you visit the graves of your fathers,' we should have said, 'Why should you tell us a lie?'

"It was good to go to the graves of our fathers. The mother went there to weep over her child: the brave went there to paint the post where lay his father. There was no place in sorrow like that where the bones of our forefathers lay. There the Great Spirit took pity on us. In our village, we were as happy as a buffalo on the plains; but now we are more like the hungry and howling wolf in the prairie.

"As the whites came nearer to us, we became more unhappy. They gave our people strong liquor, and I could not keep them from drinking it. My eldest son and my youngest daughter died. I gave away all I had; blackened my face for two years, lived alone with my family, to humble myself before the Great Spirit. I had only a piece of buffalo robe to cover me.

"White men came and took part of our lodges; and Kee-o-kuk told me I had better go West, as he had done. I said I could not forsake my village; the prophet told me I was right. I thought [73] then that Kee-o-kuk was no brave, but a coward, to give up what the Great Spirit had given us.

"The white men grew more and more; brought whiskey among us, cheated us out of our guns, our horses and our traps, and ploughed up our grounds. They treated us cruelly; and, while they robbed us, said that we robbed them. They made right look like wrong, and wrong like right. I tried hard to get right, but could not. The white man wanted my village, and back I must go. Sixteen thousand dollars every twelve moons are to be given to the Pottawatomies for a little strip of land, while one thousand dollars only was set down for our land signed away, worth twenty times as much. White man is too great a cheat for red man.

"A great chief, with many soldiers, came to drive us away. I went to the prophet, who told me not to be afraid. They only wanted to frighten us, and get our land without paying for it. I had a talk with the great chief. He said if I would go, well. If I would not, he would drive me. 'Who is Black Hawk?' said he. 'I am a Sac,' said I; 'my forefather was a Sac; and all the nation call me a Sac.' But he said I should go.

"I crossed the Mississippi with my people, during the night, and we held a council. I touched the goose quill again, and they gave us some corn, but it was soon gone. Then our women and children cried out for the roasted ears, the beans, and squashes they had been used to, and some of our braves went back in the night, [74] to take some corn from our own fields; the whites saw and fired upon them.

"I wished our great American father to do us justice. I wished to go to him with others, but difficulties were thrown in the way. I consulted the prophet, and recruited my bands to take my village again; for I knew that it had been sold by a few, without the consent of the many. It was a cheat. I said, 'I will not leave the place of my fathers.'

"With my braves and warriors, on horseback, I moved up the river, and took with us our women and children in canoes. Our prophet was among us. The great war chief, White Beaver, sent twice to tell us to go back; and that, if we did not, he would come and drive us. Black Hawk's message was this: 'If you wish to fight us, come on.'

"We were soon at war; but I did not wish it: I tried to be at peace; but when I sent parties with a white flag, some of my parties were shot down. The whites behaved ill to me, they forced me into war, with five hundred warriors, when they had against us three or four thousand. I often beat them, driving back hundreds, with a few braves, not half their number. We moved on to the Four Lakes.

"I made a dog feast before I left my camp. Before my braves feasted, I took my great medicine bag, and made a speech to my people; this was my speech: —

"'Braves and warriors! these are the medicine bags of our forefather, Muk-a-tà-quet, who was [75] the father of the Sac nation. They were handed down to the great war chief of our nation, Na-nà-ma-kee, who has been at war with all the nations of the lakes, and all the nations of the plains, and they have never yet been disgraced. I expect you all to protect them.'

"We went to Mos-co-ho-co-y-nak, where the whites had built a fort. We had several battles; but the whites so much outnumbered us, it was in vain. We had not enough to eat. We dug roots, and pulled the bark from trees, to keep us alive; some of our old people died of hunger. I determined to remove our women across the Mississippi, that they might return again to the Sac nation.

"We arrived at the Ouisconsin, and had begun crossing over, when the enemy came in great force. We had either to fight, or to sacrifice our women and children. I was mounted on a fine horse, and addressed my warriors, encouraging them to be brave. With fifty of them I fought long enough to let our women cross the river, losing only six men: this was conduct worthy a brave.

"It was sad for us that a party of soldiers from Prairie du Chien were stationed on the Ouisconsin, and these fired on our distressed women: was this brave? No. Some were killed, some taken prisoners, and the rest escaped into the woods. After many battles, I found the white men too strong for us; and thinking there would be no peace while Black Hawk was at the head of his braves, I gave myself up and my great medicine [76] bag. 'Take it,' said I. 'It is the soul of the Sac nation: it has never been dishonoured in any battle. Take it; it is my life, dearer than life; let it be given to the great American chief.'

"I understood afterwards, a large party of Sioux attacked our women, children, and people, who had crossed the Mississippi, and killed sixty of them: this was hard, and ought not to have been allowed by the whites.

"I was sent to Jefferson Barracks, and afterwards to my great American father at Washington. He wanted to know why I went to war with his people. I said but little, for I thought he ought to have known why before, and perhaps he did; perhaps he knew that I was deceived and forced into war. His wigwam is built very strong. I think him to be a good little man, and a great brave.

"I was treated well at all the places I passed through; Louisville, Cincinnati, and Wheeling; and afterwards at Fortress Monroe, Baltimore, Philadelphia, and the big village of New York; and I was allowed to return home again to my people, of whom Kee-o-kuk, the Running Fox, is now the chief. I sent for my great medicine bag, for I wished to hand it down unsullied to my nation.

"It has been said that Black Hawk murdered women and children among the whites; but it is not true. When the white man takes my hand, he takes a hand that has only been raised against warriors and braves. It has always been our custom to receive the stranger, and to use him well. The white man shall ever be welcome among us [77] as a brother. What is done is past; we have buried the tomahawk, and the Sacs and Foxes and Americans will now be friends.

"As I said, I am an old man, and younger men must take my place. A few more snows, and I shall go where my fathers are. It is the wish of the heart of Black Hawk, that the Great Spirit may keep the red men and pale faces in peace, and that the tomahawk may be buried for ever."

Austin. Poor Black Hawk! He went through a great deal. And Kee-o-kuk, the Running Fox, was made chief instead of him.

Hunter. Kee-o-kuk was a man more inclined to peace than war; for, while Black Hawk was fighting, he kept two-thirds of the tribe in peace. The time may come, when Indians may love peace as much as they now love war; and when the "peace of God which passeth all understanding" may "keep their hearts and minds in the knowledge and love of God, and of his Son Jesus Christ our Lord."

Austin. Now, just before we go, will you please to tell us a little about a buffalo hunt; just a little, and then we shall talk about it, and about Black Hawk, all the way home.

Hunter. Well, it must be a short account now; perhaps I may describe another hunt, more at length, another time. In hunting the buffalo, the rifle, the lance, and the bow and arrow are used, as the case may be. I have hunted with the Camanchees in the Mexican provinces, who are famous horsemen; with the Sioux, on the Mississippi; [78] the Crows, on the Yellow-stone river; and the Pawnees, at the Rocky Mountains. One morning, when among the Crows, a muster took place for a buffalo hunt: you may be sure that I joined them, for at that time I was almost an Indian myself.

Austin. How did you prepare for the hunt?

Hunter. As soon as we had notice, from the top of a bluff in the distance, that a herd of buffaloes was on the prairie, we prepared our horses; while some Indians were directed to follow our trail, with one-horse carts, to bring home the meat.

Brian. You were sure, then, that you should kill some buffaloes.

Hunter. Yes; we had but little doubt on that head. I threw off my cap; stripped off my coat; tying a handkerchief round my head, and another round my waist; rolled up my sleeves; hastily put a few bullets in my mouth, and mounted a fleet horse, armed with a rifle and a thin, long spear: but most of the Crows had also bows and arrows.

Basil. Your thin spear would soon be broken.

Hunter. No; these thin, long spears are sometimes used, in buffalo hunting, for years without breaking. When an Indian chases a buffalo, if he does not use his rifle or bow and arrow, he rides on fast till he comes up with his game, and makes his horse gallop just the same pace as the buffalo. Every bound his horse gives, the Indian keeps moving his spear backwards and forwards across the pommel of his saddle, with the point [79] sideways towards the buffalo. He gallops on in this way, saying "Whish! whish!" every time he makes a feint, until he finds himself in just the situation to inflict a deadly wound; then, in a moment, with all his strength, he plunges in his lance, quick as lightning, near the shoulders of the buffalo, and withdraws it at the same instant: the lance, therefore, is not broken, though the buffalo may be mortally wounded.

Brian. The poor buffalo has no chance at all.

Austin. Well! you mounted your horse, and rode off at full gallop —

Hunter. No; we walked our steeds all abreast, until we were seen by the herd of buffaloes. On catching sight of us, in an instant they set off, and we after them as hard as we could drive, a cloud of dust rising from the prairie, occasioned by the trampling hoofs of the buffaloes.

Basil. What a scamper there must be!

Hunter. Rifles were flashing, bowstrings were twanging, spears were dashed into the fattest of the herd, and buffaloes were falling in all directions. Here was seen an Indian rolling on the ground, and there a horse gored to death by a buffalo bull. I brought down one of the largest of the herd with my rifle, at the beginning of the hunt; and, before it was ended, we had as many buffaloes as we knew what to do with. Some of the party had loaded their rifles four or five times, while at full gallop, bringing down a buffalo at every fire.

Very willingly would Austin have lingered long enough to hear of half a dozen buffalo hunts; [80] but, bearing in mind what had been said about a longer account at another time, he cordially thanked the hunter for all he had told them, and set off home, with a light heart, in earnest conversation with his brothers.

Buffalo Hunt.

CHAPTER VI. [81]

The description of the buffalo hunt, given by the hunter, made a deep impression on the minds of the young people; and the manner of using the long, thin lance called forth their wonder, and excited their emulation. Austin became a Camanchee from the Mexican provinces, the Camanchees being among the most expert lancers and horsemen; Brian called himself a Sioux, from the Mississippi; and Basil styled himself a Pawnee, from the Rocky Mountains.

Many were the plans and expedients to get up a buffalo hunt upon a large scale, but the difficulty of procuring buffaloes was insurmountable. Austin, it is true, did suggest an inroad among the flock of sheep of a neighbouring farmer maintaining [82] that the scampering of the sheep would very much resemble the flight of a herd of buffaloes; but this suggestion was given up, on the ground that the farmer might not think it so entertaining an amusement as they did.

It was doubtful, at one time, whether, in their extremity, they should not be compelled to convert the chairs and tables into buffaloes; but Austin, whose heart was in the thing, had a bright thought, which received universal approbation. This was to make buffaloes of their playfellow Jowler, the Newfoundland dog, and the black tom-cat. Jowler, with his shining shaggy skin, was sure to make a capital buffalo; and Black Tom would do very well, as buffaloes were not all of one size. To work they went immediately, to prepare themselves for their adventurous undertaking, dressing themselves up for the approaching enterprise; and, if they did not succeed in making themselves look like Indians, they certainly did present a most grotesque appearance.

In the best projects, however, there is oftentimes an oversight, which bids fair to ruin the whole undertaking; and so it was on this occasion; for it never occurred to them, until they were habited as hunters, to secure the attendance of Jowler and Black Tom. Encumbered with their lances, bows, arrows and hanging dresses, they had to search the whole house, from top to bottom, in quest of Black Tom; and when he was found, a like search was made for Jowler. Both Jowler and Black Tom were at length found, and [83] led forth to the lawn, which was considered to be an excellent prairie.

No sooner was the signal given for the hunt to commence, than Black Tom, being set at liberty, instead of acting his part like a buffalo, as he ought to have done, scampered across the lawn to the shrubbery, and ran up a tree; while Jowler made a rush after him; so that the hunt appeared to have ended almost as soon as it was begun. Jowler was brought back again to the middle of the lawn, but no one could prevail on Black Tom to descend from his eminence.

Once more Jowler, the buffalo, was set at liberty; and Austin, Brian, and Basil, the Camanchee, Sioux, and Pawnee chieftains, brandished their long lances, preparing for the chase: but it seemed as though they were to be disappointed, for Jowler, instead of running away, according to the plan of the hunters, provokingly kept leaping up, first at one, and then at another of them; until having overturned the Pawnee on the lawn, and put the Sioux and Camanchee out of all patience, he lay down panting, with his long red tongue out of his mouth, looking at them just as though he had acted his part of the affair capitally.

At last, not being able to reduce the refractory Jowler to obedience, no other expedient remained than that one of them should act the part of a buffalo himself. Austin was very desirous that this should be done by Brian or Basil; but they insisted that he, being the biggest, was most like a buffalo. The affair was at length compromised, by each agreeing to play the buffalo in turn. A [84] desperate hunt then took place, in the course of which their long lances were most skilfully and effectually used; three buffaloes were slain, and the Camanchee, Sioux, and Pawnee returned in triumph from the chase, carrying a buffalo-hide (a rug mat from the hall) on the tops of their spears.

On their next visit to the hunter, they reminded him that, the last time he saw them, he had intended to speak about the prairies; but that the history of Black Hawk, and the account of the buffalo hunt, had taken up all the time. They told him that they had come early, on purpose to hear a long account; and, perhaps, he would be able to tell them all about Nikkanochee into the bargain.

The hunter replied, if that was the case, the sooner he began his narrative the better; so, without loss of time, he thus commenced his account.

Hunter. Though in our country there are dull, monotonous rivers, with thick slimy waters, stagnant swamps, and pine forests almost immeasureable in extent; yet, still, some of the most beautiful and delightful scenes in the whole world are here.

Austin. How big are the prairies? I want to know more about them.

Hunter. They extend for many hundreds of miles, though not without being divided and diversified with other scenery. Mountains and valleys, and forests and rivers, vary the appearance of the country. The name *prairie* was given to the plains of North America by the French settlers. [85] It is the French word for meadow. I will describe some prairie scenes which have particularly struck me. These vast plains are sometimes flat; sometimes undulated, like the large waves of the sea; sometimes barren; sometimes covered with flowers and fruit; and sometimes there is grass growing on them eight or ten feet high.

Brian. I never heard of such high grass as that.

Hunter. A prairie on fire is one of the most imposing spectacles you can imagine. The flame is urged on by the winds, running and spreading out with swiftness and fury, roaring like a tempest, and driving before it deer, wolves, horses, and buffaloes, in wild confusion.

Austin. How I should like to see a prairie on fire!

Hunter. In Missouri, Arkansas, Indiana, and Louisiana, prairies abound; and the whole State of Illinois is little else than a vast prairie. From the Falls of the Missouri to St. Louis, a constant succession of prairie and river scenes, of the most interesting kind, meet the eye. Here the rich green velvet turf spreads out immeasurably wide; breaking towards the river into innumerable hills and dales, bluffs and ravines, where mountain goats and wolves and antelopes and elks and buffaloes and grizzly bears roam in unrestrained liberty. At one time, the green bluff slopes easily down to the water's edge; while, in other places, the ground at the edge of the river presents to the eye an endless variety of hill and bluff and crag, taking the shapes of ramparts and [86] ruins, of columns, porticoes, terraces, domes, towers, citadels and castles; while here and there seems to rise a solitary spire, which might well pass for the work of human hands. But the whole scene, varying in colour, and lit up and gilded by the mid-day sun, speaks to the heart of the spectator, convincing him that none but an Almighty hand could thus clothe the wilderness with beauty.

Austin. Brian! Do you not wish now to see the prairies of North America?

Brian. Yes; if I could see them without going among the tomahawks and scalping-knives.

Hunter. I remember one part where the ragged [87] cliffs and cone-like bluffs, partly washed away by the rains, and partly crumbled down by the frosts, seemed to be composed of earths of a mineral kind, of clay of different colours and of red pumice stone. The clay was white, brown, yellow and deep blue; while the pumice stone, lit up by the sunbeam, was red like vermilion. The loneliness, the wildness and romantic beauty of the scene I am not likely to forget.

Basil. I should like to see those red rocks very much.

Hunter. For six days I once continued my course, with a party of Indians, across the prairie, without setting my eyes on a single tree, or a single hill affording variety to the scene. Grass, wild flowers, and strawberries, abounded more or less through the whole extent. The spot where we found ourselves at sundown, appeared to be exactly that from which we started at sunrise. There was little variety, even in the sky itself; and it would have been a relief, (so soon are we weary even of beauty itself,) to have walked a mile over rugged rocks, or to have forced our way through a gloomy pine wood, or to have climbed the sides of a steep mountain.

Brian. I hardly think that I should ever be tired of green grass and flowers and strawberries.

Hunter. Oh yes, you would. Variety in the works of creation is a gift of our bountiful Creator, for which we are not sufficiently thankful. Look at the changing seasons; how beautifully they vary the same prospect! And the changing clouds of heaven, too; what an infinite and pleasurable [88] variety they afford to us! If the world were all sunshine, we should long for the shade.

Austin. What do you mean by bluffs?

Hunter. Round hills, or huge clayey mounds, often covered with grass and flowers to the very top. Sometimes they have a verdant turf on their tops, while their sides display a rich variety of many-coloured earths, and thousands of gypsum crystals imbedded in the clay. The romantic mixture of bluffs, and hills, with summits of green grass as level as the top of a table, with huge fragments of pumice stone and cinders, the remains of burning mountains, and granite sand, and layers of different coloured clay, and cornelian, and agate, and jasper-like pebbles; these, with the various animals that graze or prowl among them, and the rolling river, and a bright blue sky, have afforded me bewildering delight. Some of the hunters and trappers believe that the great valley of the Missouri was once level with the tops of the table hills, and that the earth has been washed away by the river, and other causes; but the subject is involved in much doubt. It has pleased God to put a boundary to the knowledge of man in many things. I think I ought to tell you of Floyd's grave.

Austin. Where was it? Who was Floyd.

Hunter. You shall hear. In the celebrated expedition of Clark and Lewis to the Rocky Mountains, they were accompanied by Serjeant Floyd, who died on the way. His body was carried to the top of a high green-carpeted bluff, on the Missouri river, and there buried, and a cedar post [89] was erected to his memory. As I sat on his grave, and looked around me, the stillness and the extreme beauty of the scene much affected me. I had endured much toil, both in hunting and rowing; sometimes being in danger from the grizzly bears, and, at others, with difficulty escaping the war-parties of the Indians. My rifle had been busy, and the swan and the pelican, the antelope and the elk, had supplied me with food; and as I sat on a grave, in that beautiful bluff in the wilderness—the enamelled prairie, the thousand grassy hills that were visible, with their golden heads and long deep shadows, (for the sun was setting,) and the Missouri winding in its serpentine course, the whole scene was of the most beautiful and tranquil kind. The soft whispering of the evening breeze, and the distant, subdued and melancholy howl of the wolf, were the only sounds that reached my ears. It was a very solitary, and yet a very delightful hour.

Basil. I should not like to be by myself in such a place as that.

Hunter. There is another high bluff, not many miles from the cedar post of poor Floyd, that is well known as the burial-place of Blackbird, a famous chief of the O-ma-haw tribe; the manner of his burial was extremely strange. As I was pulling up the river, a traveller told me the story; and, when I had heard it, we pushed our canoe into a small creek, that I might visit the spot. Climbing up the velvet sides of the bluff, I sat me down by the cedar post on the grave of Blackbird. [90]

Austin. But what was the story? What was there strange in the burial of the chief?

70

Hunter. Blackbird on his way home from the city of Washington, where he had been, died with the small-pox. Before his death, he desired his warriors to bury him on the bluff, sitting on the back of his favourite war-horse, that he might see, as he said, the Frenchmen boating up and down the river. His beautiful white steed was led up to the top of the bluff, and there the body of Blackbird was placed astride upon him.

Brian. What a strange thing!

Hunter. Blackbird had his bow in his hand, his beautiful head dress of war-eagle plumes on his head, his shield and quiver at his side, and his pipe and medicine bag. His tobacco pouch was filled, to supply him on his journey to the hunting-grounds of his fathers; and he had flint and steel wherewith to light his pipe by the way. Every warrior painted his hand with vermilion, and then pressed it against the white horse, leaving a mark behind him. After the necessary ceremonies had been performed, Blackbird and his white warhorse were covered over with turf, till they were no more seen.

Austin. But was the white horse buried alive?

Hunter. He was. The turfs were put about his feet, then piled up his legs, then placed against his sides, then over his back, and lastly over Blackbird himself and his war-eagle plumes.

Brian. That was a very cruel deed! They had no business to smother that beautiful white horse in that way. [91]

Basil. And so I say. It was a great shame, and I do not like that Blackbird.

Hunter. Indians have strange customs. Now I am on the subject of prairie scenes, I ought to speak a word of the prairies on the Red River. I had been for some time among the Creeks and Choctaws, crossing, here and there, ridges of wooded lands, and tracts of rich herbage, with blue mountains in the distance, when I came to a prairie scene of a new character. For miles together the ground was covered with vines, bearing endless clusters of large delicious grapes; and then, after crossing a few broad valleys of green turf, our progress was stopped by hundreds of acres of plum trees, bending to the very ground with their fruit. Among these were interspersed patches of rose trees, wild currants, and gooseberries, with prickly pears, and the most beautiful and sweet-scented wild flowers.

Austin. I never heard of so delightful a place. What do you think of the prairies now, Basil? Should you not like to gather some of those fruits and flowers, Brian?

Hunter. And then just as I was stretching out my hand to gather some of the delicious produce of that paradise of fruit and flowers, I heard the sound of a rattlesnake, that was preparing to make a spring, and immediately I saw the glistening eyes of a copper-head, which I had disturbed beneath the tendrils and leaves.

Basil. What do you think of the prairie now, Austin? [92]

Brian. And should you not like to gather some of those fruits and flowers?

Austin. I never suspected that there would be such snakes among them.

Hunter. The wild creatures of these delightful spots may be said to live in a garden; here they pass their lives, rarely disturbed by the approach of man. The hunter and the trapper, however thoughtlessly they pursue their calling, are at times struck with the amazing beauty of the scenes that burst upon them. God is felt to be in the prairie. The very solitude disposes the mind to acknowledge Him; earth and skies proclaim his presence; the fruits of the ground declare his bounty; and, in the flowers, ten thousand forget-me-nots bring his goodness to remembrance. "Great is the Lord, and greatly to be praised; and his greatness is unsearchable." [3]

[3] Ps. cxlv. 3.

Austin. I could not have believed that there had been such beautiful places in the prairies.

Hunter. Some parts are varied, and others monotonous. Some are beautiful, and others far from being agreeable. The Prairie la Crosse, the Prairie du Chien, and the Couteau des Prairies on the Mississippi, with the prairies on the Missouri, all have some points of attraction. I did intend to say a little about Swan Lake, the wild rice grounds, Lover's Leap, the salt meadows on the Missouri, the Savannah in the Florida pine woods, and Red Pipe-stone Quarry; but as I intend to [93] give you the history of Nikkanochee, perhaps I had better begin with it at once.

Austin. We shall like to hear of Nikkanochee, but it is so pleasant to hear about the prairies, that you must, if you please, tell us a little more about them first.

Basil. I want to hear about those prairie dogs.

Brian. And I want to hear of Lover's Leap.

Austin. What I wish to hear the most, is about Red Pipe-stone quarry. Please to tell us a little about them all.

Hunter. Well! If you will be satisfied with a little, I will go on. Swan Lake is one of the most beautiful objects in the prairies of our country. It extends for many miles; and the islands with which it abounds are richly covered with forest trees. Fancy to yourselves unnumbered islands with fine trees, beautifully grouped together, and clusters of swans on the water in every direction. If you want to play at Robinson Crusoe, one of the islands on Swan Lake will be just the place for you.

Basil. Well may it be called Swan Lake.

Hunter. The first time that I saw wild rice gathered, it much surprised and amused me. A party of Sioux Indian women were paddling about, near the shores of a large lake, in canoes made of bark. While one woman paddled the canoe, the other gathered the wild rice, which flourished there in great abundance. By bending it over the canoe with one stick, and then striking it with another, the grains of rice fell in profusion into the canoe. In this way they proceeded; [94] till they obtained full cargoes of wild rice for food.

Brian. I wish we had wild rice growing in our pond.

Hunter. What I have to say of Lover's Leap is a little melancholy. On the east side of Lake Pepin, on the Mississippi, stands a bold rock, lifting up its aspiring head some six or seven hundred feet above the surface of the lake. Some years since, as the story goes, an Indian chief wished his daughter to take a husband that she did not like. The daughter declined, but the father insisted; and the poor, distracted girl, to get rid of her difficulty, threw herself, in the presence of her tribe, from the top of the rock, and was dashed to pieces.

Basil. Poor girl, indeed! Her father was a very cruel man.

Hunter. The chief was cruel, and his daughter rash; but we must not be too severe in judging those who have no better standard of right and wrong than the customs of their uncivilized tribe. It was on the Upper Missouri river, towards the mouth of the Teton river, that I came all at once on a salt meadow. You would have thought that it had been snowing for an hour or two, for the salt lay an inch or two thick on the ground.

Austin. What could have brought it there?

Hunter. The same Almighty hand that spread out the wild prairie, spread the salt upon its surface. There are salt springs in many places, where the salt water overflows the prairie. The [95] hot sun evaporates the water, and the salt is left behind.

Brian. Well, that is very curious.

Hunter. The buffaloes and other animals come by thousands to lick the salt, so that what with the green prairie around, the white salt, and the black buffaloes, the contrast in colour is very striking. Though Florida is, to a great extent, a sterile wilderness, yet, for that very reason, some of its beautiful spots appear the more beautiful. There are swamps enough, and alligators enough, to make the traveller in those weary wilds cheerless and disconsolate; but when, after plodding, day after day, through morasses and interminable pine woods, listening to nothing but the cry of cranes and the howling of wolves, he comes suddenly into an open plain covered with a carpet of grass and myriads of wild flowers, his eye brightens, and he recovers his cheerfulness and strength. He again feels that God is in the prairie.

Basil. Remember the alligators, Austin!

Brian. And the howling wolves! What do you think of them?

Hunter. The Red Pipe-stone Quarry is between the Upper Mississippi and the Upper Missouri. It is the place where the Indians of the country procure the red stone with which they make all their pipes. The place is considered by them to be sacred. They say that the Great Spirit used to stand on the rock, and that the blood of the buffaloes which he ate there ran into the rocks below, and turned them red. [96]

Austin. That is the place I want to see.

Hunter. If you go there, you must take great care of yourself; for the Sioux will be at your heels. As I said, they hold the place sacred, and consider the approach of a white man a kind of profanation. The place is visited by all the neighbouring tribes for stone with which to make their pipes, whether they are at war or peace; for the Great Spirit, say they, always watches over it, and the war-club and scalping-knife are there harmless. There are hundreds of old inscriptions on the face of the rocks; and the wildest traditions are handed down, from father to son, respecting the place. Some of the Sioux say, that the Great Spirit once sent his runners abroad, to call together all the tribes that were at war, to the Red Pipe-stone Quarry. As he stood on the top of the rocks, he took out a piece of red stone, and made a large pipe; he smoked it over them, and told them, that, though at war, they must always be at peace at that place, for that it belonged to one as much as another, and that they must all make their pipes of the stone. Having thus spoken, a thick cloud of smoke from his great red pipe rolled over them, and in it he vanished away. Just at the moment that he took the last whiff of his great, long, red pipe, the rocks were wrapped in a blaze of fire, so that the surface of them was melted. Two squaws, then, in a flash of fire, sunk under the two medicine rocks, and no one can take away red stone from the place without their leave. Where the gospel is unknown, there is nothing too improbable to be [97] received. The day will, no doubt, arrive, when the wild traditions of Red Pipe-stone Quarry will be done away, and the folly and wickedness of all such superstitions be plainly seen.

Here the hunter, having to attend his sheep, left the three brothers, to amuse themselves for half an hour with the curiosities in his cottage; after which, he returned to redeem his pledge, by relating the history he had promised them.

Indian Pipes.

CHAPTER VII. [98]

"And now," said the hunter, "for my account of Nikkanochee. [4] I met with him in Florida, his own country, when he was quite a child; indeed he is even now but a boy, being not more than twelve or thirteen years of age. The Seminole Indians, a mixed tribe, from whom prince Nikkanochee is descended, were a warlike people, settled on the banks of the River Chattahoochee. In a battle which took place between the Indians and a party of whites, under Major Dade, out of a hundred and fourteen white men, only two escaped the tomahawks of their opponents. A Seminole was about to despatch one [99] of these two, when he suddenly called to mind that the soldier had once helped him in fitting a handle to his axe. This arrested his uplifted weapon, and the life of the soldier was spared."

[4] This sketch is supposed to be a narrative of facts, though the authority for it is not within the publishers' reach.

Austin. Noble! noble! If all the Seminoles were like him, they were a noble people.

Hunter. The tribe had good and bad qualities; but I tell you this anecdote, because it affords another proof that the hardy Indian warrior, in the midst of all his relentless animosity against his enemy, is still sensible of a deed of kindness. On another occasion, when the Seminoles, to avenge injuries which their tribe had received, wasted the neighbourhood with fire and tomahawk, they respected the dwelling of one who had shown kindness to some of their tribe. Even though they visited his house, and cooked their food at his hearth, they did no injury to his person or his property. Other dwellings around it were burned to the ground, but for years his habitation remained secure from any attack on the part of the grateful Seminoles.

Basil. When I go abroad, I will always behave kindly to the poor Indians.

Hunter. The father of Nikkanochee was king of the Red Hills, in the country of the Seminoles; but not being very much distinguished as a warrior, he gave up the command of his fighting men to his brother Oseola, a chief famous for bodily strength and courage. Before the war broke out between the Seminoles, Oseola was kind and generous; but when once the war-cry had rung through the woods, and his tomahawk [100] had been raised, he became stern and implacable. He was the champion of his nation, and the terror of the pale faces opposed to him.

Brian. He must have made terrible work with his tomahawk!

Hunter. No doubt he did, for he was bold, and had never been taught to control his passions. The command of the Saviour had never reached his ears: "Love your enemies, bless them that curse you, do good to them that hate you, and pray for them which despitefully use you, and persecute you." The red man of the forest and the prairie has had much to embitter his spirit against his enemies; but I will proceed. It was in the year 1835, that between two and three hundred red warriors assembled at Camp King, to hold a "talk," or council. They were met by a battalion of white soldiers, who had two generals with them. At this council, it was proposed by the whites that a contract should be made between the two parties, wherein the Seminoles should give up their lands in Florida in exchange for other lands at a great distance from the place. Some of the red warriors were induced to make a cross on the contract as their signature, showing that they agreed therewith; but Oseola saw that such a course was bartering away his country, and sealing the ruin of his nation.

Austin. I hope he did not put his sign to it.

Brian. So do I, and I hope he persuaded all the rest of the red warriors not to sign it.

Hunter. When they asked him in his turn to sign the contract, his lip began to curl with contempt, [101] and his eye to flash with fiery indignation. "Yes!" said he, drawing a poniard from his bosom, with a haughty frown on his brow. "Yes!" said he, advancing and dashing his dagger while he spoke, not only through the contract, but also through the table on which it lay; "there is my mark!"

Austin. Well done, brave Oseola!

Brian. That is just the way that he ought to have acted.

Basil. He was a very bold fellow. But what did the generals say to him?

Hunter. His enemies, the whites, (for they were enemies,) directly seized him, and bound him to a tree. This was done in a cruel manner, for the cords cut deep into his flesh. After this, he was manacled and kept as a prisoner in solitary confinement. When it was thought that his spirit was sufficiently tamed, and that what he had suffered would operate as a warning to his people, he was set at liberty.

Austin. The whites acted a cruel part, and they ought to have been ashamed of themselves.

Brian. Yes, indeed. But what did Oseola do when he was free?

Hunter. Revenge is dear to every one whose heart God has not changed. No wonder that it should burn in the bosom of an untaught Indian. He had never heard the words of Holy Scripture, "Vengeance is mine; I will repay, saith the Lord," Rom. xii. 19; but rather looked on revenge as a virtue. Hasting to his companions, [102] he made the forest echo with the wild war-whoop that he raised in defiance of his enemies.

Brian. I thought he would! That is the very thing that I expected he would do.

Hunter. Many of the principal whites fell by the rifles of the Indians; and Oseola sent a proud message to General Clinch, telling him that the Seminoles had a hundred and fifty barrels of gunpowder, every grain of which should be consumed before they would submit to the whites. He told him, too, that the pale faces should be led a dance for five years for the indignities they had put upon him. Oseola and the Seminoles maintained the war until the whites had lost eighteen hundred men, and expended vast sums of money. At last, the brave chieftain was made prisoner by treachery.

Austin. How was it? How did they take him prisoner?

Hunter. The whites invited Oseola to meet them, that a treaty might be made, and the war brought to an end. Oseola went with his warriors; but no sooner had he and eight of his warriors placed their rifles against a tree, protected as they thought by the flag of truce, than they were surrounded by a large body of soldiers, and made prisoners.

Brian. That was an unjust and treacherous act. Oseola ought to have kept away from them.

Basil. And what did they do to Oseola? Did they kill him?

Hunter. They at first confined him in the fort at St. Augustine, and afterwards in a dungeon at [103] Sullivan's Island, near Charleston. It was in the latter place that he died, his head pillowed on the faithful bosom of his wife, who never forsook him, and never ceased to regard him with homage and affection. He was buried at Fort Moultrie, where he has a monument, inscribed "Oseola." His companions, had they been present at his grave, would not have wept. They would have been glad that he had escaped from his enemies.

Austin. Poor Oseola!

Hunter. This is only one instance among thousands, in which the red man has fallen a victim to the treachery and injustice of the whites. It is a solemn thought, that when the grave shall give up its dead, and the trumpet shall call together, face to face, the inhabitants of all nations to judgment; the deceitful, the unjust and the cruel will have to meet those whom their deceit, their injustice and cruelty have destroyed. Well may the oppressor tremble. "The Lord of hosts hath purposed, and who shall disannul it? and his hand is stretched out, and who shall turn it back?"

Basil. But you have not yet told us of Nikkanochee. Please to let us hear all about him.

Brian. Ay; we have forgotten Nikkanochee.

Hunter. I will now tell you all that I know of him; but I thought you would like to hear of his uncle, he being so famous a warrior. Nikkanochee is called Oseola Nikkanochee, prince of Econchatti, in order that he may bear in mind Oseola, his warlike uncle, and also Econchatti-mico, king of the Red Hills, his father. It is [104] thought that Nikkanochee was born on the banks of the river Chattahoochee. He can just remember the death of his mother, when he was left alone with her in a wigwam; but what I have to tell you about Nikkanochee took place during the lifetime of his father, and his uncle Oseola. The white men being at war with the Seminoles, the war-men of the latter were obliged to band themselves together to fight, leaving their squaws and children to travel as well as they could to a place of safety. Nikkanochee, child as he was, travelled with the women through the pine forests night and day; but a party of horse-soldiers overtook them, and drove them as captives towards the settlements of the whites.

Brian. Ay! now Nikkanochee is a prisoner! What is to become of him now?

Hunter. The mothers were almost frantic. The wigwams they saw on the road had been destroyed by fire, and the whole country had been devastated. At nightfall they came to a village; and here, when it grew dark, Nikkanochee, a little girl and two Indian women made their escape. For some days they fled, living on water-melons and Indian corn, till they fell in with a party of their own war-men, and among them was Nikkanochee's father.

Austin. I hope they were safe then.

Hunter. Not being numerous, they were obliged to retreat. Pursued by their enemies, they fled, sometimes on horseback, and sometimes on foot; a part of the way through the swamps, thickets and pine forests. At night, while the party were [105] sitting round a fire, in the act of preparing for refreshment some dried meat, and a wild root of the woods reduced into flour, an alarm was given. In a moment they were obliged once more to fly, for their enemies were upon their track.

Brian. Dreadful! dreadful!

Hunter. The fire was put out by the Indians, their blankets hastily rolled up, and the squaws and children sent to hide themselves in the tangled reeds and brushwood of a swamp, while the war-men turned against the enemy. The Indians beat them off, but Econchatti-mico was wounded in the wrist, a musket ball having passed through it.

Brian. Did Econchatti die of his wound?

Hunter. No; but he and the war-men, expecting that their enemies would return in greater numbers, were again forced to fly. The dreary pine forest, the weedy marsh, and the muddy swamp were once more passed through. Brooks and rapid rivers were crossed by Econchatti, wounded as he was, with his son on his back. He swam with one hand, for the other was of little use to him.

Austin. Econchatti seems to be as brave a man as Oseola. Did they escape from their enemies?

Hunter. While they were sitting down to partake of some wild turkey and deer, with which their bows and arrows had furnished them during their flight, their enemies again fell upon them. The Seminoles had, perhaps, altogether two thousand warriors, with Oseola at their head; but then the whites had at least ten thousand, to say nothing of their being much better armed. No [106] wonder that the Seminoles were compelled to fly, and only to fight when they found a favourable opportunity. But I must not dwell longer than necessary on my account; suffice it to say, that, after all the bravery of the warriors, and all the exertions of Econchatti, Nikka-nochee once more fell into the hands of the enemy.

Basil. Oh, that was terrible! I hoped he would get away safe.

Brian. So did I. I thought the white men would be tired of following them into those dreary forests and muddy swamps.

Austin. How was it that Nikkanochee was taken?

Hunter. He was captured on the 25th of August, 1836, by some soldiers who were scouring the country, and brought by them the next day to Colonel Warren. Poor little fellow, he was so worn, emaciated and cast down, that he could not be looked upon without pity. For several weeks he hardly spoke a word. No tear, no sob, nor sigh escaped him; but he appeared to be continually on the watch to make his escape. The soldiers who had taken him prisoner declared that they had followed his track full forty miles before they came up to him. From the rising to the setting of the sun they hurried on, and still he was before them. Nikkanochee must then have been only about five or six years old.

Basil. Why, I could not walk so far as forty miles to save my life. How did he manage it?

Hunter. You have not been brought up like an Indian. Fatigue and hardship and danger are endured [107] by red men from their earliest infancy. The back to the burden, Basil. You have heard the saying, "God tempers the wind to the shorn lamb." When the soldiers came up to Nikkanochee, he darted into the bushes and long grass, where they found him. At first, he uttered a scream; but, soon after, he offered the soldiers a peach which he had in his hand, that they might let him go. Placed on horseback behind one of the troopers, he was brought to the military station.

Brian. They have him now, then, fast enough. I wonder what became of Econchatti-mico, his father.

Hunter. That is not known. I should have told you that, in the Seminole language, "Econ," means hill or hills; "Chatti," is red; and the signification of "mico," is king: so that Econchatti-mico is, all together, King of the Red Hills. The soldiers who captured Nikkanochee disputed among themselves whether he ought not to be killed. Most of them were for destroying every Indian man, woman, or child they met; but one of them, named James Shields, was determined to save the boy's life, and it was owing to his humanity that Nikkanochee was not put to death.

Brian. That man deserves to be rewarded. I shall not forget James Shields.

Hunter. When Nikkanochee had afterwards become a little more reconciled to his situation, he gave some account of the way in which he was taken. He said, that as he was travelling with his father and the Indians, the white men came upon them. According to Indian custom, [108] when a party is surprised, the women and children immediately fly in different directions, to hide in the bushes and long grass, till the war-men return to them after the fight or alarm is over. Poor little Nikkanochee, in trying to cross a rivulet, fell back again into it. Besides this misfortune, he met with others, so that he could not keep up with the party. He still kept on, for he saw an old coffee-pot placed on a log; and Indians, in their flight, place things in their track, and also break off twigs from the bushes, that others of their tribe may know how to follow them. Nikkanochee came to a settlement of whites, but he struck out of the road to avoid it. He afterwards entered a peach orchard, belonging to a deserted house, and here he satisfied his hunger. It was then getting dark, but the soldiers saw him, and set off after him at full gallop. In vain he hid himself in the grass, and lay as still as a partridge, for they discovered him and took him away.

Austin. I wonder that Econchatti-mico, his father, or the brave Oseola, his uncle, did not rescue him.

Hunter. It is thought that they did return upon the back trail, for the place they had been in was shortly after surrounded by Indians, with Oseola at their head; but just then a reinforcement of soldiers arrived, and the Indians were obliged to retire. Had not the soldiers come up just in time, the whole garrison might have fallen by the rifles and scalping-knives of enraged Seminoles. Nikkanochee passed a year with the family of Colonel Warren, and was beloved by them all [109] There was, no doubt, much sympathy felt for him, as the nephew of a well-known warrior, and the son of the king of a warlike people. Nikkanochee was afterwards taken under the protection of a gentleman, who became much attached to him. He was educated with other children, and taught to bend the knee in prayer, and to offer praise to the King of kings and Lord of lords. Thus, in the providence of God, was Nikkanochee brought from being a heathen to be a worshipper of the true God and Jesus Christ.

Brian. How much longer did he remain abroad?

Hunter. A very few years, during which he became expert in climbing, swimming, loading the rifle, and using the spear. He was bold enough to attack the raccoon and otter, and was not afraid even of the alligator; few of his age were more hardy, or could bear an equal degree of fatigue. His kind protector, who adopted him as his own child, took him over to England in the year 1840. But I have given you a long account. May Nikkanochee become as celebrated for virtue and piety as his ancestors and relations were for valour and war.

Resting place for the Dead.

CHAPTER VIII. [110]

In the next visit of the three brothers to the hunter, he pointed out to them the great influence that religion had on the character of any people or country. A false religion brings with it a train of unnumbered evils; while a knowledge of the true God, and a living faith in the Saviour who died for sinners, continually promote among mankind principles of justice and kindness, and communicate to their hearts the blessings of peace and joy. "True it is," said he, "that among professedly Christian people there is much of evil; much of envy, hatred, malice, uncharitableness; of injustice, covetousness and cruelty. But this proceeds not from Christianity, but from the fallen state of human nature, which nothing but the [111] grace of God can renew, and from the great number of those who profess to be Christians, while they are uninfluenced by the gospel of the Redeemer. Christianity will neither allow us to dishonour God by bowing down to idols, nor to injure man by injustice and oppression. The Indians of our country are not found bowing down to numberless idols, as the inhabitants of many countries are: they worship what they call 'the Great Spirit,' with a deep reverence, humbling themselves before him, and undergoing self-imposed torments, to gain his good will, which the generality of Christians, in the manifestation of their faith, would find it hard to endure. They believe also in an Evil Spirit, as well as in a future state; and that they shall be happy or unhappy, just as they have done good or evil, according to their estimate of those qualities, but this belief is mixed up with mysteries and superstitions without number. I speak of Indians in the forest and the prairie, who know nothing of God's word, and who have never heard the voice of a missionary."

Hunter. The different tribes believe, that if they are expert in the chase, bold in battle, and slay many of their enemies, they shall live for ever, after death, in beautiful hunting-grounds, enjoying the pleasures of the chase continually. You know that we, as Christians, are enjoined to forgive our enemies; but untutored Indians delight in revenge: they love to boast, and to shed blood; but we are taught, by God's holy word, to be humble and merciful. There is one thing [112] that mingles much with the Indian character; and that is, medicine, or mystery. I must try to make you understand it.

Austin. Yes; I should like to know all about it very well.

Hunter. Go where you may, among the Choctaws, the Seminoles, the Crows, or the Blackfeet, every Indian has his medicine or mystery bag, which he regards with reverence, and will not part with for any price. He looks upon it as a kind of charm, or guardian spirit, that is to keep him from evil. He takes it with him to battle, and when he dies it is his companion.

Austin. But what is it? Is there any thing in the bag? What is it that makes medicine?

Hunter. Every thing that is mysterious or wonderful to an Indian, he regards as medicine. I do not mean such medicine as we get from an apothecary; but he regards it as something awful, and connected with spirits. This is a strong superstition, which has laid hold of the red man throughout the whole of his race.

Brian. But is there any thing in the medicine bag?

Hunter. The medicine bag is usually the skin of some animal, such as the beaver, otter, polecat, or weazel; or of some bird, as the eagle, the magpie, or hawk; or of some reptile, as the snake or the toad. This skin is stuffed with any thing the owner chooses to put into it, such as dry grass, or leaves; and it is carefully sewed up into some curious form, and ornamented in a curious manner. Some medicine bags are very large, [113] and form a conspicuous part of an Indian's appendages; while others are very small, and altogether hidden.

Basil. Why, it is very foolish in the red men to carry such things about with them.

Hunter. It certainly is so; but their fathers and their tribes have done so for many generations, and it would be a disgrace to them, in their own estimation, if they neglected to do the same. A young Indian, before he has his medicine bag, goes perhaps alone on the prairie, or wanders in the forest, or beside some solitary lake. Day after day, and night after night, he fasts, and calls on the Great Spirit to help him to medicine. When he sleeps, the first animal, or bird, or reptile that he dreams of, is his medicine. If it be a weazel, he catches a weazel, and it becomes his medicine for ever. If it be a toad or snake, he kills it; and if it be a bird, he shoots it, and stuffs its skin.

Austin. This is one of the most wonderful things you have told us yet.

Hunter. What is called a medicine man, or a mystery man, is one who ranks high in his tribe for some supposed knowledge. He can either make buffaloes come, or cure disease, or bring rain, or do some other wonderful things, or persuade his tribe that he can do them. Indeed, among Indians, hardly any thing is done without the medicine man. A chief, in full dress, would as soon think of making his appearance without his head as without his medicine bag. There is a saying among the Indians, that "a man lying [114] down, is medicine to the grizzly bear;" meaning, that in such a position a bear will not hurt him.

Basil. Is it true? Will not the grizzly bear hurt a man when he is lying down?

Hunter. So many people say; but I should be very sorry to trust the grizzly bear. I am afraid that he would be paying his respects to me in a very rough way.

Austin. What was it that you said about the medicine man bringing rain?

Hunter. Some of them are famous for bringing rain in a dry season.

Austin. But they cannot really bring rain.

Hunter. The matter is managed in this way. — When once they undertake to bring rain, they keep up their superstitious ceremonies, day after day, till the rain comes. Oftentimes it is very long before they succeed. It was in a time of great drought, that I once arrived at the Mandan village on the Upper Missouri. At the different Indian villages, peas and beans, wild rice, corn, melons, squashes, pumpkins, peaches and strawberries were often found in abundance; but, on this occasion, the Mandans had a very poor prospect of gathering any thing that required rain to bring it to perfection. The young and the old were crying out that they should have no green corn.

Austin. Why did they not tell the medicine men earlier to make the rain come?

Hunter. They did so: but it was not quite convenient to the medi-cine men; for they saw clearly enough that there was not the slight-est appearance [115] of rain. After putting it off, day after day, the sky grew a little cloudy to the west, when the medicine men assem-bled together in great haste to make it rain.

Brian. Ay! they were very cunning.

Hunter. No sooner was it known that the medicine men were met together in the mystery lodge, than the village was all in commo-tion. They wanted rain, and they were very sure that their medicine men could bring it when they pleased. The tops of the wigwams were soon crowded. In the mystery lodge a fire was kindled, round which sat the rain-makers, burning sweet-smelling herbs, smoking the medicine pipe, and calling on the Great Spirit to open the door of the skies, and let out the rain.

Basil. That is the way they make it rain, is it?

Hunter. At last, one of the rain-makers came out of the mystery lodge, and stood on the top of it with a spear in his hand, which he brandished about in a commanding and threatening manner, lifting it up as though he were about to hurl it up at the heavens. He talked aloud of the power of his medicine, holding up his medicine bag in one hand, and his spear in the other; but it was of no use, neither his medicine nor his spear could make it rain; and, at the setting of the sun, he came down from his elevated position in disgrace.

Austin. Poor fellow! He had had enough of rain-making for one day.

Hunter. For several days the same ceremony was carried on, until a rain-maker, with a head-dress [116] of the skins of birds, ascended the top of the mystery lodge, with a bow in his hand, and a quiver at his back. He made a long speech, which had in it much about thunder and lightning, and black clouds and drenching rain; for the sky was growing dark, and it required no great knowledge of the weather to foretell rain. He shot arrows to the east and west, and others to the north and the south, in honour of the Great Spirit who could send the rain from all parts of the skies. A fifth arrow he re-tained, until it was almost certain that rain was at hand. Then, send-ing up the shaft from his bow, with all his might, to make a hole, as he said, in the dark cloud over his head, he cried aloud for the waters to pour down at his bidding, and to drench him to the skin. He was brandishing his bow in one hand, and his medicine in the other, when the rain came down in a torrent. The whole village was clamorous with applause. He was regarded as a great mystery man, whose medicine was very powerful, and he rose to great distinction among his tribe. You see, then, the power of a mystery man in bringing rain. Does it not astonish you?

Austin. No, not a bit. I see that it was all a cheat.

Brian. I could make it rain myself as well as he did, for he never shot his arrow to pierce the cloud till it was over his head.

Hunter. To be a mystery man is regarded as a great honour; and some Indians are said to have suspended themselves from a pole, with splints through their flesh, and their medicine bags in [117] their hands, looking towards the sun, for a whole day, to obtain it.

Austin. When I go among the Indians, I will not be a mystery man.

Hunter. Now I will tell you something about Indian marriages. There is very little ceremony in an Indian marriage. The father may be seen sitting among his friends, when the young Indian comes in with presents, to induce him to give him his daughter for a wife. If the presents are not liked, they are not accepted; if they are approved, the father takes the hand of his daughter, and the hand of the young Indian, and slaps them together; after which a little feasting takes place.

Austin. Why, that is like buying a wife.

Hunter. It is; but the young Indian has already gained the good will of his intended wife: not by his fine clothes and his wealth, for he has neither the one nor the other, but by showing her the skins of the bears he has killed, and the scalps and scalp-locks of the foes he has slaughtered; and by telling her that he will hunt for her, that she may be kept from want, and fight for her, that she may be protected from the enemies of her tribe. Indians have strange customs: some flatten the heads of their young children, by laying them in a cradle, with a pillow for the back of the head, and then pressing the forehead, day after day, with a board, that comes down upon it, till the nose and forehead form a straight line. [118]

Brian. I should not like my head to be flattened in that manner.

Hunter. Children are carried about in their cradles on the backs of their mothers, wherever they go; and when children die, they are often left, in their cradles, floating on the water of a brook or pool, which their superstition teaches them to regard as sacred. A cluster of these little arks or cradles, or coffins as they may be called, of different forms, in a lone pool, is a very picturesque and affecting sight.

Basil. I shall often think of the pool, and the little cradles swimming on it. It would remind me of Moses in the bulrushes.

Hunter. There are other singular customs among the Indians. The Kowyas, the Pawnees, the Sacs and Foxes, the Osages, and the Iowas, all shave their heads, leaving a tuft on the crown two or three inches in length, and a small lock in the middle of it, as long as they can make it grow. By means of this small lock of hair braided, they ornament the tuft with a crest of the deer's tail dyed scarlet, and sometimes add to it a war-eagle's feather.

Austin. How different from the Crow Indians! They do not shave off their hair; but let it grow till it hangs down to the very ground.

Hunter. You have not forgotten that, I see. There is a cruel custom among the Indians, of exposing their aged people, that is, leaving them alone to die. If a party are obliged to remove from one place to another in search of food, and there is among them an aged man, who can no [119] longer fight, nor hunt, nor fish, nor do any thing to support himself, he is liable, although in his time he may have been a war-chief, to be left alone to die. I have seen such a one sitting by a little fire left him by his tribe, with perhaps a buffalo skin stretched on poles over his head, and a little water and a few bones within his reach. I have put my pipe to his mouth, given him pemican, and gathered sticks, that he might be able to recruit his fire; and when, months after, I have returned to the spot, there has been nothing left of him but his skeleton, picked clean by the wolves and bleaching in the winds.

Austin. This is one of the worst things we have heard of the Indians.

Basil. Oh, it is very sad indeed!

Hunter. You would not forsake your father, in old age, in that manner, would you?

Austin. No! As long as we could get a bit of bread or a drop of water, he should have part of it, and we would die with him rather than desert him.

Brian and *Basil.* Yes; that we would!

Hunter. I hope so. This is, I say, a cruel custom; but it forms a part of Indian manners, so that the old men expect it, and, indeed, would not alter it. Indians have not been taught, as we have, to honour their parents, at least not in the same way; but I can say nothing in favour of so cruel and unnatural a custom. Among the Sioux of the Mississippi, it is considered great medicine to jump on the Leaping Rock, and back again. This rock is a huge column or block, between [120] thirty and forty feet high, divided from the side of the Red Pipe-stone Quarry. It is about seven feet broad, and at a distance from the main rock of about six or eight feet. Many are bold enough to take the leap, and to leave their arrows sticking in one of its crevices; while others, equally courageous, have fallen from the top in making the attempt, and been dashed to pieces.

Brian. When you go to Pipe-stone Quarry, Austin, have nothing to do with the Leaping Rock. You must get your medicine in some other way.

Austin. I shall leave the Leaping Rock to the leaping Indians, for it will never suit me.

Hunter. There is a very small fish caught in the river Thames, called white bait, which is considered a very great luxury; but, to my taste, the white fish, of which the Chippewas take great abundance in the rapids near the Falls of St. Mary's, are preferable. The Chippewas catch them in the rapids with scoop-nets, in the use of which they are very expert. The white fish resemble salmon, but are much less in size.

Austin. The white fish of the Chippewas will suit me better than the Leaping Rock of the Sioux.

Hunter. Among the Indians, feasting, fasting, and sacrifices of a peculiar kind, form a part of their religious or superstitious observances. Some of the Pawnees, in former times, offered human sacrifices; but this cruel custom is now no more. The Mandans frequently offered a finger to the god, or Evil Spirit; and most of the tribes offer a [121] horse, a dog, a spear, or an arrow, as the case may be. Over the Mandan mystery lodge used to hang the skin of a white buffalo, with blue and black cloth of great value. These were intended as a sacrifice or an offering to the good and evil spirits, to avert their anger and to gain their favour.

Brian. How many things you do remember!

Hunter. All the chiefs of the tribes keep runners: men swift of foot, who carry messages and commands, and spread among the people news necessary to be communicated. These runners sometimes go great distances in a very short space of time.

Brian. You must have your runners, Austin.

Austin. Oh yes, I will have my runners: for I shall want pipe-stone from Red Pipe-stone Quarry, and white fish from the Chippewas; and then I shall send messages to the Cherokees and Choctaws, the Camanchees, the Blackfeet and the Crows.

Hunter. The squaws, or wives of the Indians, labour very contentedly, seeming to look on servitude as their proper calling. They get in wood and water; they prepare the ground for grain, cook victuals, make the dresses of their husbands, manufacture pottery, dress skins, attend to the children, and make themselves useful in a hundred other ways.

Brian. I think the squaws behave themselves very well.

Hunter. The smoking of the pipe takes place [122] on all great occasions, just as though the Indians thought it was particularly grateful to the Good and Evil Spirits. In going to war, or in celebrating peace, as well as on all solemn occasions, the pipe is smoked. Oftentimes, before it is passed round, the stem is pointed upwards, and then offered to the four points—east, west, north and south. In the hands of a mystery man, it is great and powerful medicine. If ever you go among the red men, you must learn to smoke; for to refuse to draw a whiff through the friendly pipe offered to you, would be regarded as a sad affront.

Basil. What will you do now, Austin? You never smoked a pipe in your life.

Austin. Oh, I should soon learn; besides, I need only take a very little whiff.

Hunter. You must learn to eat dog's flesh, too; for when the Indians mean to confer a great honour on a chief or a stranger, they give him a dog feast, in which they set before him their most favourite dogs, killed and cooked. The more useful the dogs were, and the more highly valued, the greater is the compliment to him in whose honour the feast is given; and if he were to refuse to eat of the dog's flesh, thus prepared out of particular respect to him, no greater offence could be offered to his hospitable entertainers.

Brian. You have something a little harder to do now, I think, Austin; to learn to eat dog's flesh.

Austin. You may depend upon it, that I shall keep out of the way of a dog feast. I might take [123] a little whiff at their pipe, but I could not touch their dainty dogs.

Hunter. In some of the large lodges, I have seen very impressive common life-scenes. Fancy to yourselves a large round lodge, holding ten or a dozen beds of buffalo skins, with a high post between every bed. On these posts hang the shields, the war-clubs, the spears, the bows and quivers, the eagle-plumed head-dresses, and the medicine bags of the different Indians who sleep there; and on the top of each post the buffalo mask, with its horns and tail, used in the buffalo dance. Fancy to yourselves a group of Indians in the middle of the lodge, with their wives and their little ones around them, smoking their pipes and relating their adventures, as happy as ease and the supply of all their animal wants can make them. While you gaze on the scene, so strange, so wild, so picturesque and so happy, an emotion of friendly feeling for the red man thrills your bosom, a tear of pleasure starts into your eye; and, before you are aware, an ejaculation of thankfulness has escaped your lips, to the

Father of mercies, that, in his goodness and bounty to mankind, he has not forgotten the inhabitants of the forest and the prairie.

The Indians have a method of hardening their shields, by smoking them over a fire, in a hole in the ground; and, usually, when a warrior thus smokes his shield, he gives a feast to his friends. Some of the pipes of the Indians are beautiful. The bowls are all of the red stone from Pipe-stone Quarry, cut into all manner of fantastic [124] forms; while the stems, three or four feet long, are ornamented with braids of porcupine's quills, beaks of birds, feathers and red hair. The calumet, or, as it is called, "the peace-pipe," is indeed, as I have before said, great medicine. It is highly adorned with quills of the war-eagle, and never used on any other occasion than that of making and solemnizing peace, when it is passed round to the chiefs. It is regarded as altogether a sacred utensil. An Indian's pipe is his friend through the pains and pleasures of life; and when his tomahawk and his medicine bag are placed beside his poor, pallid remains, his pipe is not forgotten.

Austin. When an Indian dies, how do they bury him?

Hunter. According to the custom of his tribe. Some Indians are buried under the sod; some are left in cots, or cradles, on the water; and others are placed on frames raised to support them. You remember that I told you of Blackbird's grave.

Austin. Ay! he was buried on horseback, on the top of a high bluff, sitting on his horse. He was covered all over with sods.

Hunter. And I told you of the Chinock children floating on the solitary pool.

Basil. Yes, I remember them very well.

Hunter. Grown-up Chinocks are left floating in cradles, just in the same manner; though oftener they are tied up in skins, and laid in canoes, with paddles, pipes and provisions, and then hoisted up into a tree, and left there to decay. In the [125] Mandan burial place, the dead were ranged in rows, on high slender frames, out of the way of the wolf, dressed in their best robes, and wrapped in a fresh buffalo skin, with all their arms, pipes, and every necessary provision and comfort to supply their wants in their journey to the hunting-grounds of their fathers. In our burial grounds, there are generally some monuments grander than the rest, to set forth the wealth, the station, or the talents of those who slumber below; and, as human nature is the same everywhere, so in the resting place of the Indians. Here and there are spread out a few yards of red or blue cloth, to signify that beneath it a chief, or a superior brave, is sleeping. The Mandan dead occupied a spot on the prairie. Here they mouldered, warrior lying by the side of warrior, till they fell to the ground from their frames, when the bones were buried, and the skulls ranged with great care, in round rings, on the prairie, with two buffalo skulls and a medicine pole in the centre.

Austin. Ay! it would be of no use for the wolf to come then, for there would be nothing for him. I should very much like to see an Indian burying-place.

Hunter. Were you to visit one, you would see that the heart and affections are at work under a red skin, as well as under a white one; for parents and children, husbands and wives, go there to lament for those who are dear to them, and to humble themselves before the Great Spirit, under whose care they believe their departed relatives to be. The skulls, too, are visited, and every [126] one is placed carefully, from time to time, on a tuft of sweet-smelling herb or plant. Life is but a short season with both the white and the red man, and ought to be well spent. It is as a flower that flourishes: "For the wind passeth over it, and it is gone; and the place thereof shall know it no more." But I have now told you enough for the present. Come again, as soon as you will; I shall have some anecdotes of Indians ready for you.

Indian Cradle.

CHAPTER IX. [127]

With willing feet, sparkling eyes and happy hearts, Austin and his two brothers again set off for the cottage near the wood. On an ordinary occasion, they might have found time for a little pleasant loitering; but the Indian anecdotes they expected to hear excited their curiosity too much to allow a single minute to be lost. A pin might have been heard falling on the ground, when, seated in the cottage, they listened to the following anecdotes of the hunter.

Hunter. It has pleased God to endue Indians with quick perceptions. They are amazingly quick in tracing an enemy, both in the woods and the prairie. A broken twig or leaf, or the faintest impression on the grass, is sufficient to attract their [128] attention. The anecdotes I am about to relate are believed to be true, but I cannot myself vouch for their correctness, having only read them, or heard them related by others.

An Indian, upon his return home to his hut one day, discovered that his venison, which had been hung up to dry, had been stolen. After going some distance, he met some persons, of whom he inquired if they had seen a *little, old, white man*, with a short gun, and accompanied by a small dog with a bob-tail. They replied in the affirmative; and, upon the Indian's assuring them that the man thus described had stolen his venison, they desired to be informed how he was able to give such a minute description of a person whom he had not seen. The Indian answered thus: —

"The thief I know is a *little* man, by his having made a pile of stones in order to reach the venison, from the height I hung it standing on the ground; that he is an *old* man, I know by his short steps, which I have traced over the dead leaves in the woods; that he is a *white* man, I know by his turning out his toes when he walks, which an Indian never does; his gun I know to be short, by the mark which the muzzle made by rubbing the bark of the tree on which it leaned; that the dog is small, I know by his tracks; and that he has a bob-tail, I discovered by the mark of it in the dust where he was sitting at the time his master was taking down the meat."

Brian. Well done, Indian! Why, nothing could escape a man like that. [129]

Austin. An Englishman would hardly have been able to describe the thief without seeing him.

Hunter. You shall have another instance of the quick perceptions of the red men. A most atrocious and shocking murder was once committed, by a party of Indians, on fourteen white settlers, within five miles of Shamokin. The surviving whites, in their rage, determined to take their revenge by murdering a Delaware Indian, who happened to be in those parts, and who was far from thinking himself in any danger. He was a great friend to the whites, was loved and esteemed by them, and, in testimony of their regard, had received from them the name of Duke Holland, by which he was generally known.

This Indian, satisfied that his nation were incapable of committing such a foul murder in a time of profound peace, told the enraged settlers that he was sure the Delawares were not in any manner concerned in it, and that it was the act of some wicked Mingoes or Iroquois, whose custom it was to involve other nations in wars with each other, by secretly committing murders, so that they might appear to be the work of others. But all his representations were vain; he could not convince exasperated men, whose minds were fully bent on revenge.

At last, he offered that, if they would give him a party to accompany him, he would go with them in quest of the murderers, and was sure that he could discover them by the prints of their feet, and other marks well known to him, by which he [130] would convince them that the real perpetrators of the crime belonged to the Six Nations.

His proposal was accepted. He marched at the head of a party of whites and led them into the tracks. They soon found themselves in the most rocky part of a mountain, where not one of those who accompanied him could discover a single track, nor would they believe that men had ever trodden on this ground, as they had to jump from rock to rock, or to crawl over them. They began to believe that the Indian had led them across these rugged mountains in order to give the enemy time to escape. They threatened him with instant death the moment they should be convinced of the fraud.

The Indian, true to his promise, took pains to make them perceive that an enemy had passed along the places through which he was leading them. Here, he showed them that the moss on the road had been trodden down by the weight of a human foot; there, that it had been torn and dragged forward from its place. Again, he would point out to them, that pebbles, or small stones on the rocks, had been removed from their beds by the foot hitting against them; that dry sticks, by being trodden upon, were broken; and, in one particular place, that an Indian's blanket had been dragged over the rocks, and had removed or loosened the leaves lying there, so that they did not lie flat, as in other places. All these marks the Indian could perceive as he walked along, without even stopping.

At last, arriving at the foot of the mountain, on [131] soft ground, where the tracks were deep, he found that the enemy were eight in number; and, from the freshness of the foot-prints, he concluded that they must be encamped at no great distance.

This proved to be the exact truth; for, after gaining the eminence on the other side of the valley, the Indians were seen encamped: some having already laid down to sleep, while others were drawing off their leggings, or Indian stockings, for the same purpose, and the scalps they had taken were hanging up to dry.

"See," said Duke Holland to his astonished companions, "there is the enemy; not people of my nation, but Mingoes, as I truly told you. They are in our power. In less than half an hour they will be all fast asleep. We need not fire a gun, but go up and tomahawk them. We are nearly two to one, and need apprehend no danger. Come on, and you will now have your full revenge."

But the whites, overcome with fear, did not choose to follow the Indian's advice, but desired him to take them back by the nearest and best way. This he did; and when they arrived at home, they reported the enemy to have been so great that they durst not venture to attack them.

Austin. This instance is quite as wonderful as the other.

Brian. I would not have an Indian after me if I had done wrong; for he would be sure to find me out.

Hunter. Red men often act very conscientiously. One day, an Indian solicited a little tobacco [132] of a white man, to fill his pipe. Having some loose in his pocket, the white man gave him a handful. The next day the Indian returned in search of the man who had given him the tobacco.

"I wish to see him," said the Indian.

"Why so?" inquired some one.

"Why, I find money with the tobacco."

"Well! what of that? Keep it; it was given to you."

"Ah!" said the Indian, shaking his head, "I got good man and bad man here," pointing to his breast. "Good man say, 'Money not yours; you must return it:' bad man say, ''Tis yours; it was given to you.' Good man say, 'That not right: *tobacco* yours, *money* not yours.' Bad man say, 'Never mind, nobody know it; go buy rum.' Good man say, 'Oh no; no such thing.' So poor Indian know not what to do. Me lie down to sleep, but no sleep; good man and bad man talk all night, and trouble me. So now, me bring money back: now, me feel good."

Basil. I like that Indian very much.

Brian. No one could have acted more honestly.

Hunter. Whatever the Indians may be, when oppressed, wronged and deceived by the whites; and however they may act towards their enemies; they are usually honest towards their own tribe. While I was residing on the Big Beaver, says one who lived much among them, I passed by the door of an Indian who was a trader, and had, consequently, a quantity of goods in his house. He was going with his wife to Pittsburg, and they were shutting up the house; as no person [133] remained in it during their absence. This shutting up was nothing else than putting a large block, with a few sticks of wood, outside against the door, so as to keep it closed. As I was looking at this man with attention, while he was so employed, he addressed me in these words:—

"See, my friend, this is an Indian lock that I am putting to my door."

I answered, "Well enough; but I see you leave much property in the house: are you not afraid that those articles will be stolen while you are gone?"

"Stolen! by whom?"

"Why, by Indians, to be sure."

"No, no," replied he, "no Indian would do such a thing. Unless a white man, or white people, should happen to come this way, I shall find all safe on my return."

Basil. If we were to leave our doors in that way, our houses would be sure to be robbed.

Hunter. No doubt they would; but Indians have good and bad qualities. The notion entertained by the Iroquois Indians, respecting the creation of mankind, will show how ignorant they are with respect to the Creator of all things; but, indeed, if the blessed book of truth were not in our hands, we should be equally ignorant ourselves. Before man existed, say they, there were three great and good spirits; of whom one was superior to the other two, and is emphatically called the Great Spirit and the Good Spirit. At a certain time, this exalted being said to one of the others, "Make a man." He obeyed; and, [134] taking chalk, formed a paste of it, and moulding it into the human form, infused into it the animating principle, and brought it to the Great Spirit. He, after surveying it, said, "This is too white."

He then directed the other to make a trial of his skill. Accordingly, taking charcoal, he pursued the same process, and brought the result to the Great Spirit; who, after surveying it, said, "It is too black."

Then said the Great Spirit, "I will now try myself;" and taking red earth, he formed an Indian. On surveying it, he said, "This is a proper or perfect man."

After relating the strange opinion of the Iroquois Indians, the hunter advised the young people, on their return home, to look over the account of the creation of the world and mankind, in the first chapter of Genesis; telling them that they could not be too thankful for the opportunity of reading God's word, which was not only sufficient to keep them from error in such things, but was able also to make them "wise unto salvation through faith which is in Christ Jesus." He told them, that though the Indians were ignorant of holy things, they did not want shrewdness and sagacity. "When General Lincoln," said he, "went to make peace with the Creek Indians, one of the chiefs asked him to sit down on a log; he was then desired to move, and, in a few minutes, to move still farther. The request was repeated, until the general got to the end of the log. The Indian still said, 'Move farther;' to which the [135] general replied, 'I can move no farther.' 'Just so it is with us,' said the chief. 'You have moved us back to the water, and then ask us to move farther!'"

In the account of his expedition to the foot of the Rocky Mountains, in 1821, Major Long relates the following anecdote of a Pawnee brave, son of Red Knife, who, in the succeeding winter, visited the city of Washington, during the session of Congress.

This brave, of fine size, figure and countenance, is now about twenty-five years old. At the age of twenty-one, his heroic deeds had acquired for him in his nation the rank of the bravest of the braves. The savage practice of torturing and burning to death their prisoners existed in this nation. An unfortunate female, of the Paduca nation, taken in war, was destined to this horrid death.

The fatal hour had arrived. The trembling victim, far from her home and her friends, was fastened to the stake. The whole tribe were assembled on the surrounding plains to witness the awful scene.

Just as the funeral pile was to be kindled, and the whole multitude of spectators were on the tiptoe of expectation, this young warrior, having, unnoticed, prepared two fleet horses, with the necessary provisions, sprang from his seat, rushed through the crowd, liberated the victim, seized her in his arms, placed her on one of the horses, mounted the other himself, and made the utmost speed towards the nation and friends of the captive. [136]

The multitude, dumb and nerveless with amazement at the daring deed, made no effort to rescue their victim from her deliverer.

They viewed it as the immediate act of the Great Spirit, submitted to it without a murmur, and quietly retired to their village.

The released captive was accompanied three days through the wilderness, towards her home. Her deliverer then gave her the horse on which she rode, and the necessary provisions for the remainder of the journey, and they parted.

On his return to the village, such was his popularity, that no inquiry was made into his conduct, and no censure was passed upon it. Since this transaction no human sacrifice has been offered in this or any other of the Pawnee tribes; the practice is abandoned. How influential is one bold act in a good cause! This deed illustrates a grand principle, boys. It is by such men that great reformations are made in the world, and yet there is no mastery in it. Every one is capable of doing that which he knows to be right, regardless of the opinions of wicked men, or the habits of the weak and foolish, who follow customs which have no apology but that others have done so before.

The publication of this anecdote at Washington led some young ladies, in a manner highly creditable to their good sense and good feeling, to present this brave and humane Indian with a handsome silver medal, with appropriate inscriptions, as a token of their sincere commendation of the noble act of rescuing one of their sex, [137] an innocent victim, from a cruel death. Their address, delivered on this occasion, is sensible and appropriate, closing as follows:

"Brother—Accept this token of our esteem; always wear it for our sakes; and when again you have the power to save a poor woman from death and torture, think of this, and of us, and fly to her relief and rescue."

To this the Pawnee made the following reply:—

"Brothers and sisters—This medal will give me ease more than I ever had; and I will listen more than I ever did to white men.

"I am glad that my brothers and sisters have heard of the good deed that I have done. My brothers and sisters think that I have done it in ignorance, but I now know what I have done.

"I did do it in ignorance, and I did not know that I did good; but by your giving me this medal I know it."

The cruelty of torturing and burning a captive, the great danger of the female Indian, and the noble daring of the Pawnee brave, formed the subject of conversation for some time among the young people; and Austin was unbounded in his approbation of the Pawnee. Willingly would he have contributed towards another silver medal for him, and Brian and Basil would not have been backward in doing their part; but the affair appeared hardly practicable, inasmuch as a reasonable doubt existed whether the Pawnee brave was still alive; and, even if he were, there seemed to be no direct way of communicating with him.

Indian Horsemanship. — Page 160.

CHAPTER X. [138]

"Remember," said Austin, as he urged his brothers to quicken their pace on their way to the cottage, "we have hardly heard any thing yet about buffaloes and grizzly bears, and other animals which are found in the woods and the prairie. Let us make haste, that we may have a long visit."

Brian and Basil, being almost as anxious as their brother to hear all about bears and buffaloes, quickened their pace as he desired them, so that no long period had passed, before the hunter, at the request of his youthful visitors, was engaged in giving them the desired account.

"The different animals and birds," said he, "that inhabit different countries, for the most part, [139] roam backwards and forwards, according to the season. Creatures that love the cold move northerly in summer, and such as delight in a warmer clime move southerly in winter. It is, however, principally to obtain food that they remove from one place to another. I must here explain to you, that though I have, in common with most others who use these terms, spoken of buffaloes, the animal which abounds in the prairie is not properly the buffalo, but the bison."

Austin. But if they are bisons, why are they called buffaloes?

Hunter. That is a question that I hardly know how to answer. From whatever cause it may have arisen, certain it is, that the name of buffalo has become common; and, that being the case, it is used in conversation, and oftentimes in books, as being more easily understood.

Brian. What is the difference between a buffalo and a bison?

Hunter. A buffalo is an animal that abounds in Africa, resembling an ugly cow, with a body long, but rather low; and very long horns. But the bison stands very high in front, has a hump on the back part of the neck covered with long hair, short horns, and a profusion of long shaggy hair hanging from its head, neck and fore-legs.

Austin. Then a bison must look much fiercer than a buffalo.

Hunter. He does; and from the circumstance of his fore-parts standing high, while he carries his head low, he always appears as if he were about to run at you. Bisons abound throughout [140] the whole of our country, west of the Mississippi; but the reckless way in which they are slaughtered, and the spread of civilization, are likely, in a few years, greatly to decrease their numbers. Indians suffer much from hunger, but they are very reckless when buffaloes are plentiful. On one occasion, when among the Minatarees, I witnessed a grand capture of buffaloes. It was effected by different parties taking different directions, and then gradually approaching each other. The herd was thus hemmed in on all sides, and the slaughter was terrible. The unerring rifle, the sharp spear and the winged arrow, had full employ; and so many buffaloes were slain, that, after taking their tongues and other choice parts of them for food, hundreds of carcasses were left for the prairie-wolves to devour. Thus it is that man, whether savage or civilized, too often becomes prodigal of the abundance he enjoys, and knows not the value of what he possesses, till taught by that want into which his thoughtless waste has plunged him.

Austin. Ay, they will soon kill all the buffaloes, if they go on in that manner.

Hunter. At present, they are to be seen on the prairie in droves of many thousands; the woods, also, abound with them; and often, in the heat of summer, an incalculable number of heads and horns are visible in the rivers, the bodies of the bisons being under the water.

Brian. What, because they are so hot?

Hunter. Yes: the bison suffers very much from heat. It is no uncommon thing to see a bison bull [141] lay himself down in a puddle of water, and turn himself round and round in it, till he has half covered his body with mud. The puddle hole which he thus makes is called a bison or buffalo wallow. The puddle cools him while he is in it, and when he quits it, the mud plastered on his sides defends him from the burning heat of the sun.

Basil. What a figure a bison bull must cut, with his shaggy hair and his sides plastered all over with mud!

Hunter. Bears are often most formidable foes to the hunter; but there is this striking difference between the common bear and the grizzly bear, that while the former eats mostly vegetables, and will do his best to get out of your way, the latter eats nothing but flesh, and is almost sure to attack you. Hunters and Indians make it a rule never to fire at a grizzly bear, unless in self-defence: except in cases when they have a strong party, or can fire from a tree; for, when he is wounded, his fury knows no bounds.

Austin. How can you escape from a grizzly bear, if he is so very terrible?

Hunter. The common bear can climb a tree, as I have already told you; but the grizzly bear is no climber. If you have time to get up into a tree, you are safe: if not, you must reserve your shot till the animal is near you, that you may take a steady aim. You must then fight it out in the best way you can. Grizzly bears are sometimes of a very large size, measuring from nine to ten feet in length. It was on the Upper Missouri that [142] I was once chased by one of these terrible fellows, and a narrow escape I had.

Austin. How was it? Tell us all about it.

Hunter. I had just fired off my rifle at a bird which I took for an eagle, little thinking how soon my wasted bullet (for I did not strike the bird) would be wanted in defence of my life. The crack of my piece reverberated from the green-topped bluffs that rose from the prairie; and I suppose it was this that brought Sir Bruin upon me. He came on with huge strides, and I had nothing but a hunting-knife to use in my defence, my discharged rifle being of no use. There was no tree near, so throwing down my piece, I drew my knife as a forlorn hope in my extremity.

Austin. A hunting-knife against a grizzly bear!

Hunter. When the huge monster was within a few yards of me, to my amazement, I heard the report of two rifles, and in the same instant my tremendous foe fell, with two bullets in his head. This timely assistance was rendered me by two of our party, who, having followed my track, were near me when I thought myself alone.

Austin. Never was any one in greater danger.

Hunter. I will tell you an anecdote that I have read of a common bear. A boy, about eight years old, was sent by his mother into the woods, to bring home the old cow. At the distance of somewhat more than half a mile, he found her, attended by some young cattle. He began to drive them home; but had not proceeded far, when a bear came out of the bushes, and seemed disposed to make his acquaintance. [143]

The boy did not like his company; so he jumped upon the old cow's back, and held on by her horns. She set out at full speed, and the bear after her. The young cattle, lifting their tails in the air, brought up the rear. Thus they proceeded, the young ones behind frequently coming up to the bear, and giving him a thrust with their horns.

This compelled him to turn round, and thus the old cow, with her brave rider, got somewhat in advance. The bear then galloped on, and, approaching the boy, attempted to seize him; but the old cow cantered along, and finally brought the boy to his mother's house in safety. The bear, thinking he should not be welcome there, after approaching the house, turned about and scampered back to the forest. Sir Bruin knew when he was well off; a whole skin is the best covering a bear can have; but, if he ventures among mankind, he is likely enough to have it stripped over his ears.

Austin. That was a capital old cow, for she saved the boy's life.

Basil. But the young cattle helped her, for they pushed the bear with their horns.

Brian. Please to tell us about wild horses.

Hunter. The hordes or bands of wild horses that abound in some of the prairies, are supposed to be the offspring of Spanish horses, brought to Mexico by Europeans. They are extremely shy, keen in their sight and swift of foot, so that to come up with them, except by surprise, is no easy thing. I have seen them in great numbers from [144] the brow of a bluff, or have peeped at them cautiously from a ravine.

Austin. What kind of horses are they; and of what colour?

Hunter. Some of them are fine animals, but in general they are otherwise. Stunted and coarse in appearance, they are of various colours — bay, chestnut, cream, gray, piebald, white and black, with long tails, fetlocks, top-knots and manes.

Brian. How do they catch them?

Hunter. In different ways. Sometimes a well-mounted Indian, armed with his rifle, follows a horde of horses, until he can get a fair shot at the best among them. He aims at the top of the neck, and if he succeeds in striking the high gristle there, it stuns the animal for the moment, when he falls to the ground without being injured. This is called *creasing* a horse: but a bad marksman would kill, and not crease, the noble animal he seeks to subdue.

Austin. What other way is there of catching wild horses? for that seems to be a very bad one.

Basil. It is a very bad way. They ought not to shoot them.

Hunter. They are much more commonly taken with the *lasso;* which is a thong at least a dozen yards long, ending in a noose. This the Indians throw, at full gallop, over the head of the flying steed they wish to secure. Rarely do they miss their aim. When a horse is thus caught, the hunter leaps from his steed, and lets out the lasso gradually, choking his captive till he is obliged to stop: he then contrives to hopple or tie his fore-legs; [145] to fasten the lasso round his lower jaw; to breathe in his nostrils, and to lead him home.

Austin. Breathe in his nostrils! Why, what does he do that for?

Hunter. Because experience has taught him, that it does much towards rendering his captive more manageable. It is said, that if an Indian breathes freely into the nostrils of a wild young buffalo on the prairie, the creature will follow him with all the gentleness and docility of a lamb.

Brian. Well! that does appear strange!

Hunter. There is one animal, which the Indians, the hunters and trappers sometimes meet with, that I have not mentioned. It is the cougar, or panther, or American lion; for it goes by all these names. Now and then it is to be seen in the thick forests of the west; but, being a sad coward, it is not so much dreaded as it otherwise would be.

Brian. I should not much like to meet a cougar.

Hunter. The common wolf of America is as big as a Newfoundland dog, and a sulky, savage-looking animal he is. So long as he can feed in solitary places he prefers to do so, but, when hunger-pressed, he attacks the fold; after which, Mr. Grizzly-skin loses no time in getting to a place of shelter, for he knows that should he outrun the stanch hounds that will soon be on his track, yet will a rifle ball outrun him.

Brian. Yes, yes; Mr. Grizzly-back is very cunning.

Hunter. The prairie-wolf is smaller than the common wolf. Prairie-wolves hunt after deer [146] which they generally overtake; or keep close to a buffalo herd, feeding on such as die, or on those that are badly wounded in fighting with one another. The white, black, and clouded wolves are in the northern parts. There are many kinds of deer. I told you, that sometimes a deer-hunt took place on a large scale, by enclosing a circle, and driving the deer into it. In shooting antelopes, the hunter has only to stick up his ramrod in the ground in their neighbourhood, and throw over it his handkerchief; while he, with his rifle ready loaded, lies on the grass near at hand. The antelopes will soon approach the handkerchief to see what it is, when the hunter may make them an easy prey. The largest deer is the moose deer, which is often seven feet high. He is an awkward, overgrown-looking creature, with broad horns; but, awkward as he is, I question if any of you could outrun him. Mountain and valley, lake and river, seem alike to him, for he crosses them all. In the snow, to be sure, the unwearied and persevering hound will overtake him; but let him beware of his horns, or he will be flying head over heels in the air in a twinkling. The moose deer, however, cannot successfully strive with the hunter's rifle.

Austin. Nothing can stand against man.

Hunter. And yet what is man opposed to his Maker? His strength is perfect weakness! In a moment, in a twinkling of an eye, he "changes his countenance, and sends him away."

Basil. What other kinds of deer do Indians catch? [147]

The Wapiti Deer.

Hunter. The elk, with his large branching horns, who would despise a palace as a dwelling-place. Nothing less than the broad sky above his head, and the ground of the boundless forest beneath his feet, will satisfy him. After the elk, come the Virginia, or common deer, the wapiti deer, the black-tailed deer, and the cariboo. All these are the prey of the hunter. Their savoury flesh supplies him with food, and their soft skins are articles of merchandise. The mountain sheep may often be seen skipping from one ledge to another of the rugged rocks, and precipitous clayey [148] cliffs of the western wilds, giving life to the solitary place, and interest to the picturesque beauty of lonely spots.

Austin. You have mentioned all the animals now, I think, that the hunter chases; for you spoke before about beavers, badgers, foxes, raccoons, squirrels and some others.

Basil. You have never told us, though, how they catch the musk-rat. I should like to know that.

Hunter. Well, then, I will tell you how they take the musk-rat, but must first speak about the prairie dog. Prairie dogs are a sort of marmot, but their bark is somewhat like that of a small dog. Rising from the level prairie, you may sometimes see, for miles together, small hillocks of a conical form, thrown up by the prairie dogs, which burrow some eight or ten feet in the ground. On a fine day, myriads of these dogs, not much unlike so many rats, run about, or sit barking on the tops of their hillocks. The moment any one approaches them, they disappear, taking shelter in their burrows.

Basil. Oh, the cunning little rogues.

Hunter. The musk-rat builds his burrow (which looks like a hay-stack) of wild rice stalks; so that, while he has a dry lodging, a hole at the bottom enables him, when he pleases, to pass into the shallow water beneath his burrow or lodge. In taking a musk-rat, a person strikes the top of the burrow, and out scampers the tenant within; but no sooner does he run through his hole into the shallow water, than he is instantly caught [149] with a spear. Myriads of these little animals are taken in this manner for their fur.

Brian. They must be a good deal like prairie dogs, though one has his house on the land, and the other in the water.

Hunter. These wide prairies, on which roam bisons and horses and deer innumerable; and these shallow waters, where musk-rats abound, will probably, in succeeding years, assume another character. White men will possess them; civilized manners and customs will prevail, and Christianity spread from the Mississippi to the Rocky Mountains; for the kingdoms of the world, you know, are to become the kingdoms of our Lord and of his Christ.

Austin. You have told us a great deal indeed, to-day, about the prairies.

Hunter. I have already spoken of the prairie fires; I mean the burning grass set on fire by accident, or purposely, for the double advantage of obtaining a clearer path and an abundant crop of fresh grass; but I must relate an adventure of my own, of a kind not likely to be forgotten. So long as a prairie fire is confined to the high grounds, there is very little danger from it; for, in such situations, the grass being short, the fire never becomes large, though the line of flame is a long one. Birds and beasts retire before it in a very leisurely manner; but in plains where the grass is long, it is very different.

Austin. I should like to see one of those great, high, round bluffs on fire. There must be a fine bonfire then. [150]

Hunter. There you are mistaken, for as I have already told you, the grass is short on the bluffs. To be sure, the sight of a bluff on fire, on a dark night, is very singular; for as you can only see the curved line of flame, the bluff being hidden by the darkness, so it seems as though the curved lines of flame were up in the air, or in the sky.

Basil. They must look very beautifully.

Hunter. They do: but when a fire takes place in a low bottom of long grass, sedge and tangled dry plants, more than six feet high; and when a rushing wind urges on the fiery ruin, flashing like the lightning and roaring like the thunder; the appearance is not beautiful, but terrible. I have heard the shrill war-whoop, and the clash of contending tomahawks in the fight, when no quarter has been given. I have witnessed the wild burst where Niagara, a river of waters, flings itself headlong down the Horseshoe Fall; and I have been exposed to the fury of the hurricane. But none of these are half so terrible as the flaming ocean of a long-grass prairie-fire.

Austin. Oh! it must be terrible.

Hunter. The trapper is bold, or he is not fit for his calling; the hunter is brave, or he could never wage war as he does with danger; and the Indian from his childhood is familiar with peril: yet the Indian, the hunter and the trapper tremble, as well they may, at a prairie-meadow fire. But I must relate my adventure.

Basil. I am almost afraid to hear it.

Austin. Poh! nonsense! It will never hurt you. [151]

Hunter. A party of five of us, well mounted, and having with us our rifles and lances, were making the best of our way across one of the low prairie bottoms, where the thick coarse grass and shrubs, even as we sat on our horses, were often as high as our heads; when we noticed, every now and then, a flight of prairie hens, or grouse, rapidly winging their way by us. Two of our party were of the Blackfoot tribe; their names were Ponokah (elk) and Moeese (wigwam.) These Indians had struck into a buffalo trail, and we had proceeded for a couple of hours as fast as the matted grass and wild pea-vines would allow, when suddenly the wind that was blowing furiously from the east became northerly, and in a moment, Moeese, snuffing the air, uttered the words, "Pah kapa," (bad;) and Ponokah, glancing his eyes northward, added, "Eehcooa pah kaps," (very bad.)

Austin. I guess what was the matter.

Brian. And so do I.

Hunter. In another instant a rush was heard, and Ponokah, who was a little ahead, cried out, "Eneuh!" (buffalo!) when three bisons came dashing furiously along another trail towards us. No sooner did they set eyes on us, than they abruptly turned southward. By this time, we all understood that, to the north, the prairie was on fire; for the air smelt strong. Deer, and bisons, and other animals, sprang forward in different directions from the prairie, and a smoke, not very distant, like a cloud, was visible.

Austin. I hope you set off at full gallop. [152]

Hunter. We were quite disposed to urge our horses onward; but the trail took a turn towards the burning prairie, and we were obliged to force our way into another, in doing which my horse got his feet entangled, and he fell, pitching me over his head some yards before him. I was not hurt by the fall, for the thick herbage protected me; but the worst of it was, that my rifle, which had been carelessly slung, fell from my shoulder among the long grass, and being somewhat confused by my fall, I could not find it.

Brian. You ought not to have stopped a moment.

116

Hunter. Perhaps not; but, to a hunter, a rifle is no trifling loss, and I could not make up my mind to lose mine. Time was precious, for the smoke rapidly increased; and both Ponokah and Moeese, who knew more about burning prairies than I did, and were therefore more alive to our danger, became very impatient. By the time my rifle was found, and we were ready to proceed, the fire had gained upon us in a crescent form, so that before and behind we were hemmed in. The only point clear of the smoke was to the south; but no trail ran that way, and we feared that, in forcing a road, another accident might occur like that which had befallen us.

Austin. I cannot think what you could do in such a situation.

Hunter. Our disaster had come upon us so unexpectedly, and the high wind had so hurried on the flaming storm, that there seemed to be no time for a moment's thought. Driven by necessity, [153] we plunged into the thick grass to the south; but our progress was not equal to that of the fire, which was now fast approaching, blackening the air with smoke, and roaring every moment louder and louder. Our destruction seemed almost certain; when Ponokah, judging, I suppose, by the comparative thinness of the smoke eastward, that we were not far from the boundary of the prairie bottom, dashed boldly along a trail in that direction, in the face of the fire, crying out to us to follow. With the daring of men in extremity, we put our horses to their speed, broke through the smoke, fire, grass, and flame, and found ourselves almost instantly on a patch of ground over which the fire had passed; but, as the grass had evidently been scanty, we were free from danger. From a neighbouring bluff, which the smoke had before hidden from our view, we saw the progress of the flame — a spectacle that filled me with amazement. The danger we had escaped seemed increased by the sight of the fearful conflagration, and I know not whether terror, amazement, or thankfulness most occupied my mind.

Austin. That was, indeed, a narrow escape.

Hunter. As we stood on the bluff, dismounted, to gaze on the flying flames — which appeared in the distance like a huge fiery snake of some miles in length, writhing in torture — my wonder increased. The spectacle was fearful and sublime, and the conflagration nearest to us resembled the breakers of the deep that dash on a rocky shore, only formed of fire, roaring and destroying, preceded by thick clouds of smoke. Before then, I [154] had been accustomed to sights and scenes of peril, and had witnessed the burning of short grass to some extent; but this was the first time I had been in such fearful danger—the first time I felt the awfulness of such a situation—the first time that I had really seen the prairie on fire!

Brian. There can be nothing in the world like a burning prairie, unless it be a burning mountain.

Hunter. A burning prairie, when we are near it, is a vast and overwhelming spectacle; but every rising and setting sun exhibits Almighty wisdom, power and goodness, on a scale infinitely beyond that of a hundred burning prairies. It is a good thing to accustom ourselves to regard the works of creation around us with that attention and wonder they are calculated to inspire, and especially to ponder on the manifestation of God's grace set forth in his holy word. When burning prairies and burning mountains shall be all extinguished; when rising and setting suns and all earthly glory shall be unknown; then shall the followers of the Redeemer gaze on the brighter glories of heaven, and dwell for ever with their Leader and their Lord.

Buffalo Dance.

CHAPTER XI. [155]

Buffaloes, bears, wild horses, wolves, deer, prairie-dogs and musk-rats, were a fruitful source of conversation to the young people in their leisure hours, until such time as they could again visit their interesting friend at the cottage. Various plans were formed to attack grizzly bears, to catch wild horses, and to scare away half-famished wolves; in all of which, Jowler, notwithstanding his bad behaviour at the buffalo hunt, was expected to act a distinguished part. Black Tom was scarcely considered worth thinking about, he being too wild by half for a wild horse, and too faint-hearted for a grizzly bear. At one time, it was so far determined for him to play the part of a prairie-dog, that Austin set about digging a hole [156] for him: before it was finished, however, the plan was abandoned; Brian and Basil both feeling positive that, let Austin dig a hole as deep as he would, Black Tom would never be persuaded to run into it.

After much deliberation, catching wild horses being given up—on the score that Black Tom would run away too fast, and Jowler would not run a way at all—a bear hunt was resolved on, having, as Brian observed, two especial advantages: the first, that all of them could enjoy the sport at once; and the second, that Jowler would be sure to attack them all, just like a grizzly bear.

No time was lost in preparing their long spears, and in dressing themselves as much like renowned chiefs as their knowledge and resources would allow. And, in order that Jowler might the more closely resemble a grizzly bear, a white apron was spread over his broad back, and tied round his neck. The lawn was, as before, the scene of their exploits, the prairie on which the fearful monster was to be overcome; and, to the credit of their courage be it spoken, neither Austin, Brian nor Basil, manifested the slightest token of fear.

Jowler was led by them among the bushes of the shrubbery, that he might burst out upon them all at once; and this part of the arrangement answered excellently well, only that Jowler arrived on the prairie first instead of last; add to which, the bushes having so far despoiled him of his grizzly hide, the white apron, as to have pulled it off his back, he set to work mouthing and tearing at it, to get it from his neck. At last, in spite of a few [157] untoward and unbearlike actions on the part of Jowler, the attack took place. With undaunted resolution, Austin sustained Jowler's most furious charges; Brian scarcely manifested less bravery; and little Basil, though he had broken his lance, and twice fallen to the earth, made a desperate and successful attack on his fearful antagonist, and caught him fast by the tail. It was on the whole a capital adventure; for though they could not with truth say that they had killed the bear, neither could the bear say that he had killed them.

The bear hunt being at an end, they set off for the cottage; for the hunter had promised to describe to them some of the games of the Indian tribes, and he was soon engaged in giving them an account of the ball-play of the Choctaws. "At the Choctaw ball-play thousands of spectators attend, and sometimes a thousand young men are engaged in the game."

Hunter. It is played in the open prairie, and the players have no clothes on but their trowsers, a beautiful belt formed of beads, a mane of dyed horse-hair of different colours, and a tail sticking out from behind like the tail of a horse; this last is either formed of white horse-hair or of quills.

Brian. And how do they play?

Hunter. Every man has two sticks, with a kind of hoop at the end, webbed across, and with these they catch and strike the ball. The goal on each side, consisting of two upright posts and a pole across the top, is set up twenty-five feet high; these goals are from forty to fifty rods apart. Every time either party can strike the ball [158] through their goal, one is reckoned, and a hundred is the game.

Basil. What a scuffle there must be among so many of them!

Hunter. When every thing is ready for the game to begin, a gun is fired; and some old men, who are to be the judges, fling up the ball in the middle, half-way between the two goals.

Brian. Now for the struggle.

Hunter. One party being painted white, every man knows his opponent. No sooner is the ball in the air, than a rush takes place. Every one with his webbed stick raised above his head; no one is allowed to strike or to touch the ball with his hands. They cry out aloud at the very top of their voices, rush on, leap up to strike the ball, and do all they can to help their own side and hinder their opponents. They leap over each other, dart between their rivals' legs, trip them up, throw them down, grapple with two or three at a time, and often fall to fisticuffs in right earnest. There they are, in the midst of clouds of dust, running, striking and struggling with all their might; so that, what with the rattle of the sticks, the cries, the wrestling, the bloody noses, the bruised shins, the dust, uproar and confusion, such a scene of excitement is hardly to be equalled by any other game in the world.

Brian. How long does the game last?

Hunter. It begins about eight or nine o'clock in the morning, and sometimes is scarcely finished by sunset. A minute's rest is allowed every time the ball is urged beyond the goal, and then the [159] game goes on again till it is finished. There is another ball-play somewhat resembling this, which is played by the women of the Prairie du Chien, while the men watch the progress of the game, or lounge on the ground, laughing at them.

Austin. Do they ever run races?

Hunter. Yes, and very expert they are. Many of the tribes are extravagantly fond of horses. You see an Indian, with his shield and quiver, his ornamented shirt, leggins, and mocassins; his long hair flowing behind him, or his head-dress of the war-eagle tailing gracefully nearly to his heels; his lance in his hand; and his dress ornamented with ermine, shells, porcupine quills and a profusion of scalp-locks; but you see him out of character. He should spring on a horse wild as the winds; and then, as he brandished his lance, with his pendent plumes, and hair and scalp-locks waving in the breeze, you see him in his proper element. Horse-racing among the Indians is an exciting scene. The cruel custom, of urging useful and noble animals beyond their strength, is much the same in savage as in civilized life; but the scene is oftentimes more wild, strange, and picturesque than you can imagine.

Austin. Ay, I remember that the Camanchees are capital riders. I was a Camanchee in our buffalo hunt. Brian, you have not forgotten that?

Brian. But you had no horse to ride. I was a Sioux; and the Sioux are capital riders too.

Basil. And so are the Pawnees, I was a Pawnee in the buffalo hunt.

Hunter. It was told me that the Camanchees—and, [160] indeed, some of the Pawnees also—were able, while riding a horse at full gallop, to lie along on one side of him, with an arm in a sling from the horse's neck, and one heel over the horse's back; and that, while the body was thus screened from an enemy, they could use their lances with effect, and throw their arrows with deadly aim. The Camanchees are so much on their horses, that they never seem at their ease except when they are flying across the prairie on horse-back.

Austin. It would be worth going to the prairies, if it were only to see the Camanchees ride.

Hunter. Besides horse-races, the Indians have foot-races and ca-noe-races and wrestling. The Indians are also very fond of archery, in which, using their bows and also arrows so much as they do, it is no wonder they are very skilful. The game of the arrow is a very favourite amusement with them. It is played on the open prairie. There is no target set up to shoot at, as there is generally; but every archer sends his first arrow as high as he can into the air.

Austin. Ay, I see! He who shoots the highest in the air is the win-ner.

Hunter. Not exactly so. It is not he who shoots highest that is the victor; but he who can get the greatest number of arrows into the air at the same time. Picture to yourselves a hundred well-made, active young men, on the open prairie, each carrying a bow, with eight or ten arrows, in his left hand. He sends an arrow into the air with all his strength, and then, instantly, with a [161] rapidity that is truly surprising, shoots arrow after arrow upwards, so that, before the first arrow has reached the ground, half a dozen others have mounted into the air. Often have I seen seven or eight shafts from the same bow in the air at once.

Austin. Brian, we will try what we can do to-morrow; but we shall never have so many as seven or eight up at once.

Hunter. The Indians are famous swimmers, and, indeed, if they were not, it would often go hard with them. They are taught when very young to make their way through the water, and though they do it usually in a manner different from that of white men, I hardly think many white men would equal them, either as to their speed, or the length of time they will continue in the water.

Austin. But how do they swim, if their way is different from ours? I can swim a little, and I should like to learn their way, if it is the best.

Hunter. I am not quite prepared to say that; for, though red men are more expert swimmers than white men, that may be owing to their being more frequently in the water. They fish a great deal in the lakes; and they have often to cross brooks and rivers in too much haste to allow them to get into a canoe. A squaw thinks but very little of plunging into a rolling river with a child on her back; for the women swim nearly or quite as well as the men.

Austin. But you did not tell us wherein their way of swimming is different from ours.

Hunter. Whites swim by striking out their legs [162] and both arms at the same time, keeping their breasts straight against the water; but the Indian strikes out with one arm only, turning himself on his side every stroke, first on one side and then on the other, so that, instead of his broad chest breasting the water in front, he cuts through it sideways, finding less resistance in that way than the other. Much may be said in favour of both these modes. The Indian mode requires more activity and skill, while the other depends more on the strength of the arms, a point in which they far surpass the Indian, who has had little exercise of the arms, and consequently but comparatively little strength in those limbs. I always considered myself to be a good swimmer, but I was no match for the Indians. I shall not soon forget a prank that was once played me on the Knife River, by some of the Minatarees; it convinced me of their adroitness in the water.

Basil. What was it? Did they dip your head under the water?

Hunter. No; you shall hear. I was crossing the river in a bull-boat, which is nothing more than a tub, made of buffalo's skin, stretched on a framework of willow boughs. The tub was just large enough to hold me and the few things which I had with me; when suddenly a group of young swimmers, most of them mere children, surrounded me, and began playfully to turn my tub round and round in the stream. Not being prepared to swim, on account of my dress, I began to manifest some fear lest my poor tub should be [163] overturned; but the more fearful I was, the better pleased were my mirthful tormentors.

Austin. Ah! I can see it spinning round like a peg-top, in the middle of the river.

Brian. And did they upset the tub?

Hunter. No. After amusing themselves for some time at my expense, now and then diving under the tub, and then pulling down the edge of it level with the water, on receiving a few beads, or other trifles which I happened to have with me, they drew me and my bull-boat to the shore in safety. They were beautiful swimmers, and, as I told you, I shall not soon forget them.

The dances among the Indians are very numerous; some of them are lively enough, while others are very grave; and, then, most of the tribes are fond of relating adventures.

There are the buffalo dance, the bear dance, the dog dance and the eagle dance. And then there are the ball-play dance, the green corn dance, the beggars' dance, the slave dance, the snow-shoe dance, and the straw dance; and, besides these, there are the discovery dance, the brave dance, the war dance, the scalp dance, the pipe-of-peace dance, and many others that I do not at this moment remember.

Brian. You must please to tell us about them all.

Austin. But not all at once, or else we shall have too short an account. Suppose you tell us of two or three of them now.

Hunter. To describe every dance at length [164] would be tiresome, as many of them have the same character. It will be better to confine ourselves to a few of the principal dances. I have known a buffalo dance continue for a fortnight or longer, day and night, without intermission. When I was among the Mandans, every Indian had a buffalo mask ready to put on whenever he required it. It was composed of the skin of a buffalo's head, with the horns on it; a long, thin strip of the buffalo's hide, with the tail at the end of it, hanging down from the back of the mask.

Austin. What figures they would look with their masks on! Did you say that they kept up the dance day and night?

Hunter. Yes. The Mandans were strong in their village, but comparatively weak whenever they left it, for then they were soon in the neighbourhood of their powerful enemies. This being the case, when the buffaloes of the prairie wandered far away from them, they were at times half starved. The buffalo dance was to make buffaloes come back again to the prairies near them.

Brian. But how could they bring them back again?

Hunter. The buffalo dance was a kind of homage paid to the Great Spirit, that he might take pity on them, and send them supplies. The dancers assembled in the middle of the village, each wearing his mask, with its horns and long tail, and carrying in his hand a lance, or a bow and arrows. The dance began, by about a [165] dozen of them thus attired, starting, hopping, jumping and creeping in all manner of strange, uncouth forms; singing, yelping, and making odd sounds of every description, while others were shaking rattles and beating drums with all their might; the drums, the rattles, the yelling, the frightful din, with the uncouth antics of the dancers, altogether presented such a scene, that, were you once to be present at a buffalo dance, you would talk of it long after, and would not forget it all the days of your lives.

Basil. And do they keep that up for a fortnight?

Hunter. Sometimes much longer, for they never give over dancing till the buffaloes come. Every dancer, when he is tired, (and this he makes known by crouching down quite low,) is shot with blunt arrows, and dragged away, when his place is supplied by another. While the dance is going on, scouts are sent out to look for buffaloes, and as soon as they are found, a shout of thanksgiving is raised to the Great Spirit, to the medicine man, and to the dancers, and preparation is made for a buffalo hunt. After this, a great feast takes place; all their sufferings from scarcity are forgotten, and they are as prodigal, and indeed wasteful, of their buffalo meat, as if they had never known the want of it.

Austin. Well, I should like to see the buffalo dance. Could not we manage one on the lawn, Brian?

Brian. But where are we to get the buffalo masks from? The buffalo hunt did very well, [166] but I hardly think we could manage the dance Please to tell us of the bear dance.

Hunter. I think it will be better to tell you about that, and other dances, the next time you visit me; for I want to read to you a short account, which I have here, of a poor Indian woman of the Dog-ribbed tribe. I have not said much of Indian women, and I want you to feel kindly towards them. It was Hearne, who went with a party from Hudson's Bay to the Northern Ocean, many years ago, who fell in with the poor woman.

Basil. Oh, yes; let us hear all about her; and you can tell us of the dances when we come again.

Hunter. Now, then, I will begin. One day in January, when they were hunting, they saw the track of a strange snow-shoe, which they followed, and at a considerable distance came to a little hut, where they discovered a young woman sitting alone. On examination, she proved to be one of the Dog-ribbed Indians, who had been taken prisoner by another tribe, in the summer of 1770; and, in the following summer, when the Indians that took her prisoner were near this place, she had escaped from them, intending to return to her own country. But the distance being so great, and having, after she was taken prisoner, been carried in a canoe the whole way, the turnings and windings of the rivers and lakes were so numerous that she forgot the track; so she built the hut in which she was found, to protect her from the weather during the winter, and here she had resided from the first setting-in of the fall. [167]

Brian. What, all by herself! How lonely she must have been!

Hunter. From her account of the moons passed since her escape, it appeared that she had been nearly seven months without seeing a human face; during all which time she had supplied herself very well, by snaring partridges, rabbits and squirrels: she had also killed two or three beavers, and some porcupines. She did not seem to have been in want, and had a small stock of provisions by her when she was discovered. She was in good health and condition, and one of the finest of Indian women.

Austin. I should have been afraid that other Indians would have come and killed her.

Hunter. The methods practised by this poor creature to procure a livelihood were truly admirable, and furnish proof that necessity is indeed the mother of invention. When the few deer sinews, that she had an opportunity of taking with her, were expended, in making snares and sewing her clothing, she had nothing to supply their place but the sinews of the rabbits' legs and feet. These she twisted together for that purpose with great dexterity and success. The animals which she caught in those snares, not only furnished her with a comfortable subsistence, but of the skins she made a suit of neat and warm clothing for the winter. It is scarcely possible to conceive that a person in her forlorn situation could be so composed as to be capable of contriving and executing any thing that was not absolutely necessary to her existence; but there was sufficient [168] proof that she had extended her care much farther, as all her clothing, besides being calculated for real service, showed great taste, and exhibited no little variety of ornament. The materials, though rude, were very curiously wrought, and so judiciously placed, as to make the whole of her garb have a very pleasant, though rather romantic appearance.

Brian. Poor woman! I should like to have seen her in the hut of her own building, and the clothes of her own making.

Hunter. Her leisure hours from hunting had been employed in twisting the inner rind or bark of willows into small lines, like net-twine, of which she had some hundred fathoms by her. With these she intended to make a fishing-net, as soon as the spring advanced. It is of the inner bark of the willows, twisted in this manner, that the Dog-ribbed Indians make their fishing-nets; and they are much preferable to those made by the Northern Indians.

Five or six inches of an iron hoop, made into a knife, and the shank of an arrow-head of iron, which served her as an awl, were all the metals this poor woman had with her when she escaped; and with these implements she had made herself complete snow-shoes, and several other useful articles.

Austin. Capital! Why, she seems able to do every thing.

Hunter. Her method of making a fire was equally singular and curious, having no other materials for that purpose than two hard stones. [169] These, by long friction and hard knocking, produced a few sparks, which at length communicated to some touch-wood. But as this method was attended with great trouble, and not always successful, she did not suffer her fire to go out all the winter.

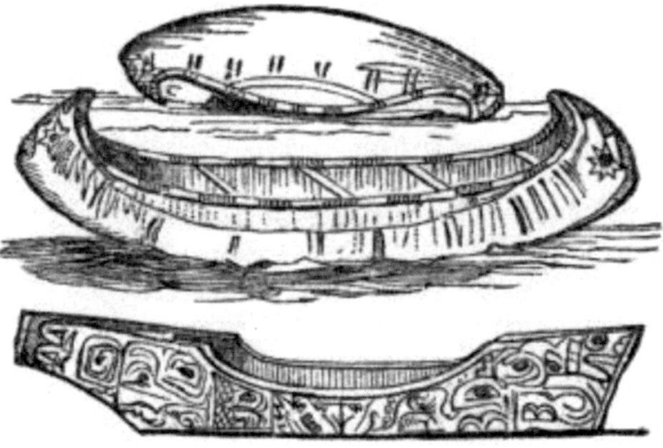

Indian Canoes.

c, drum. d, d, rattles. e, drum. f, mystery whistle. g, deer-skin flute.

CHAPTER XII. [170]

Never, sure, did young people make a more grotesque appearance, than did Austin, Brian, and Basil Edwards, in their attempt to get up a buffalo dance. Each had a mat over his shoulders, and a brown paper mask over his face; two wooden pegs on a string made a very respectable pair of horns; bows and arrows were in abundance; a toy rattle and drum, with the addition of an iron spoon and a wooden trencher, supplied them with music; and neither Mandan, Pawnee, Crow, Sioux, Blackfoot, nor Camanchee, could have reasonably complained of the want of either noise or confusion.

Then, again, they were very successful in bringing buffaloes, without which the dance, excellent as it was, would have been but an unsatisfactory [171] affair. Black Tom had been prudently shut up in the tool-house, and Jowler tied up to a tree hard by, so that, when it became expedient for buffaloes to appear, the house of Black Tom was opened, and Jowler was set at liberty. All things considered, the affair went off remarkably well.

"We are come to hear of the bear dance, and the dog dance, and the beggars' dance, and the green corn dance," said Austin to the hunter, on the following day, when a visit was paid to the cottage. The hunter, with his accustomed kindness to the young people, lost no time in entering on his narrative. "You must not forget," said he, "that many of the dances of the Indians partake of a religious character, for in them reverence and adoration are freely offered. The Indians' worship of the Great Spirit, as I have already told you, is mingled with much of ignorance and superstition, whether in dances or in other observances; yet do they, at times, leave upon the mind of a spectator a deep impression of their sincerity, though this does not excuse their error. I have not as yet described their music, and therefore will do it now."

Austin. Yes. Now for the music of the Indians, if you please, sir.

Hunter. If you ever go among them, and mingle in their dances, you must not expect to have a band of music such as you have in our cities. Whistles, flutes, rattles and drums are almost all their musical instruments. You would be surprised at the music that some of the young Indians produce with the mystery whistle. [172]

Austin. Why is it called the mystery whistle?

Hunter. I have already told you that the red man calls every thing mystery, or medicine, that is surprising; and as the notes of this whistle are particularly sweet, it may be called a mystery whistle on this account. There is another whistle that is very much in request among the Indians, and that is the war whistle. The onset and the retreat in battle are sounded on this instrument by the leading chief, who never goes on an expedition without it. It is made of bone, and sometimes it is formed of the leg bone of a large bird. The shrill, scream-like note, which is the signal for rushing on an enemy, would make you start.

Brian. What sort of a drum do they use? Is it a kettle-drum?

Hunter. No. It is merely a piece of raw hide, stretched as tight as it can be pulled over a hoop. Some of their drums have but one end, or surface, to beat upon, while others have two. What they would do in their dances without their drums I do not know, for you hear them continually. Their rattles are of different kinds, some much larger than others; but the principle on which they are formed is the same, that is, of enclosing stones of different sizes in hard, dry, raw hide.

Austin. Have they no trumpets and cymbals, and clarionets and violins?

Hunter. No, nothing of the kind. They have a deer-skin flute, on which very tolerable music is sometimes made; but, after all, it must be admitted that Indians are much better buffalo hunters than musicians. [173]

Austin. Ay; they are quite at home in hunting buffaloes.

Hunter. Yes; and they are at home, too, in dancing, being extremely nimble of foot. Some of their dances are so hideous that you would be disgusted with them, while others would keep you laughing in spite of yourselves.

Brian. You must please to tell us about these dances.

Hunter. Dancing is a very favourite amusement of the Indians; though it is, for the most part, of a character so different from that of dancing in civilized life, that few people, ignorant of its meaning and allusions, would like it. The body is so continually in a stooping attitude, and the gestures and grimaces appear to be so unmeaning, that at first it leaves an impression that they are ridiculing the art of dancing, rather than entering into it in right earnest. There is such creeping and jumping and starting, that a spectator can make but little of it.

Austin. I can fancy that I see a party joining in the buffalo dance now, with their masks over their faces. Please to tell us of the bear dance.

Hunter. By and by. I will describe a few other dances first. The beggars' dance is undertaken to prevail on such of the spectators as abound in comforts to give alms to those who are more scantily provided with them. It is danced by the young men who stand high in the tribe. These shake their rattles, hold up their pipes and brandish their lances, while they dance; chanting in an odd strain, at the top of their voices, in [174] praise of the Great Spirit, and imploring him to dispose the lookers on to give freely. The dancers are all naked, with the exception of a sort of kilt formed of quills and feathers; and a medicine man keeps on all the time beating furiously on a drum with a rattle, and hallooing out as loud as he can raise his voice.

Austin. That ought to be called the begging dance, and not the beggars' dance; for the dancers do not beg for themselves, but for others.

Hunter. You see that the object of the dance is a good one; for many a skin, or pouch, or pipe, or other necessary article, is given by the spectators to those of their tribe who need them. It is not common among the Indians for their aged men and mystery men to mingle in the dance, and yet I have seen, on especial occasions, a score of them jumping and capering in a way very creditable to their agility. The Sioux have a dance that ought to be called the doctors' dance, or the dance of the chiefs.

Brian. Why, do the doctors dance in it?

Hunter. Yes; while a medicine man beats his drum, and a party of young women sing, the chiefs of the tribe and the doctors make their appearance, splendidly attired in their costliest head-dresses, carrying a spear in one hand and a rattle in the other. Every movement is strictly regulated by the beat of the drum, and the dance by degrees becomes more and more spirited, until you would suppose the party must be exhausted: but men so much in the open air, and whose limbs are so little restrained by bandages and tight clothing, [175] can bear a great deal of fatigue. The pipe dance is one of the most animated amusements.

Basil. Oh! do tell us about the pipe dance.

Hunter. In the ground in the centre of the village a fire is lighted, and a party assemble round it; every one smoking his pipe, as he sits on his buffalo skin, as though nothing was farther from his thoughts than dancing. While these are whiffing away at a distance from the fire, a mystery man, who sits nearer to the flame, smokes a longer pipe, grunting at the same time a kind of tune. Suddenly is heard the rub-a-dub of a drum, or the beat of some other instrument of the same kind; when instantly starts to his feet one of the smokers, hopping like a parched pea, spinning round like a top, and starting and jumping, at every beat of the drum, in a very violent manner. In this way he goes round the smokers, seemingly threatening them all, and at last pounces upon one of them, whom he compels to dance in the same manner as himself. The new dancer acts his part like the former one, capering and jumping round the smokers, and compelling another to join them. Thus the dance continues, till all of them are occupied, when the hopping, the jumping, the frightful postures into which they throw themselves, together with the grunting, growling, singing, hooting and hallooing, are beyond all belief. There are few dances of the Indians more full of wild gestures and unrestrained turbulence than the pipe dance.

Basil. I hope you have a good many more dances to tell us of. [176]

Hunter. The green corn dance of the Minatarees must be described to you. Among Indian tribes, green corn is a great luxury, and the time when it ripens is a time of rejoicing. Dances and songs of thanksgiving are abundant; and the people give way not only to

136

feasting, but also to gluttony; so that often, by abusing the abundance in their possession, they bring upon themselves the miseries of want. The Indians have very little fore-thought. To enjoy the present, and to trust the future to the Great Spirit, is their constant practice.

Austin. How long does the green corn dance last?

Hunter. For eight or ten days, during which time there is the most unbounded prodigality. Among many of the tribes, the black drink, a very powerful medicine, is taken two or three days before the feast, that the green corn may be eaten with a sharp appetite and an empty stomach.

Brian. In what way does the green corn dance begin?

Hunter. As soon as the corn is in a proper state—and this is decided by the mystery men—runners are despatched through the village, that all may assemble on the following day to the dance and the feast. Sufficient corn for the required purpose is gathered by the women, who have the fields under their care, and a fire is made, over which a kettle, with green corn in it, is kept boiling; while medicine men, whose bodies are strangely painted, or bedaubed with clay of a white colour, dance round it in very uncouth attitudes, with corn-stalks in their hands. [177]

Austin. I dare say, while the pot is boiling, they are all longing to begin the feast.

Hunter. The first kettle-full is not for themselves, it is an offering to the Great Spirit. There are many customs among the Indians which cannot but bring the Jews to our remembrance; and this offering of the first green corn does so very forcibly. The medicine men round the fire shake their rattles, hold up their corn-stalks, and sing loudly a song of thanksgiving, till the corn is sufficiently boiled; it is then put upon the fire and consumed to a cinder. Before this offering is made, none of the Indians would dare to taste of the luxurious fare; but, afterwards, their appetite is unrestrained.

Austin. Then they begin to boil more corn, I suppose.

Hunter. A fresh fire is made, a fresh kettle of corn is prepared, and the dance goes on; the medicine men keeping close to the fire, and the others capering and shouting in a larger circle, their energy increasing as the feast approaches nearer and nearer. The chiefs and medicine men then sit down to the feast, followed by the whole tribe, keeping up their festivity day after day, till the corn-field has little more grain remaining in it than what is necessary for seed. You have heard the saying, "Wilful waste brings woful want." The truth of this saying is often set forth, as well in civilized life as among the Indians.

Basil. I wonder what dance will come next.

Hunter. I need not describe many others. If I run rapidly through two or three, and dwell a [178] little on the bear dance and the war dance, you will then have heard quite enough about dances. The scalp dance is in use among the Sioux or Dahcotas. It is rather a fearful exhibition; for women, in the centre of a circle, hold up and wave about the scalps which have been torn from the slaughtered foes of the tribe, while the warriors draw around them in the most furious attitudes, brandishing their war-clubs, uttering the most hideous howls and screams. The Indians have many good qualities, but cruelty seems to mingle with their very nature. Every thing is done among them that can be done, to keep alive the desire to shed blood. The noblest act a red man can perform, and that which he thinks the most useful to his tribe and the most acceptable to the Great Spirit, is to destroy an enemy, and to bear away his scalp as a trophy of his valour. If it were only for this one trait in the Indian character, even this would be sufficient to convince every humane person, and especially every Christian, of the duty and great advantage of spreading among them the merciful principles of Christianity. A holy influence is necessary to teach the untutored red man to forgive his enemies, to subdue his anger, to abate his pride, and to stay his hand in shedding human blood. The new commandment must be put in his heart: "That ye love one another." The Mandan boys used to join in a sham scalp dance, in which they conducted themselves just like warriors returning from a victorious enterprise against their enemies.

Basil. They are all sadly fond of fighting. [179]

Hunter. In the brave dance, of the Ojibbeways, there is plenty of swaggering: the dancers seem as if they knew not how to be proud

138

enough of their warlike exploits. The eagle dance, among the Choctaws, is an elegant amusement; and the snow-shoe dance, of the Ojibbeways, is a very amusing one.

Brian. Please to tell us about them both.

Hunter. I must not stay to describe them particularly: it will be enough to say, that, in the one, the dancers are painted white, and that they move about waving in their hands the tail of the eagle; in the other—which is performed on the first fall of snow, in honour of the Great Spirit—the dancers wear snow-shoes, which, projecting far before and behind their feet, give them in the dance a most strange and laughable appearance.

Brian. I should very much like to see that dance; there is nothing cruel in it at all.

Basil. And I should like to see the eagle dance, for there is no cruelty in that either.

Hunter. The straw dance is a Sioux dance of a very curious description. Loose straws are tied to the bodies of naked children; these straws are then set on fire, and the children are required to dance, without uttering any expression of pain. This practice is intended to make them hardy, that they may become the better warriors.

Basil. That is one of the strangest dances of all.

Hunter. I will now say a little about the bear dance, and the war dance. The bear dance is performed by the Sioux before they set off on a bear-hunt. If the bear dance were left unperformed, [180] they would hardly hope for success. The Bear spirit, if this honour were not paid to him, would be offended, and would give them no success in the chase.

Austin. What! do the Sioux think there is a Bear spirit?

Bear Dance.

Hunter. Yes. The number of spirits of one kind or another, believed in by the Indians, is very great. In the bear dance, the principal performer has a bear-skin over him, the head of it hanging over his head, and the paws over his hands. Others have masks of bears' faces; and all of them, throughout the dance, imitate the actions of a bear. They stoop down, they dangle their hands, and make frightful noises, beside singing to the Bear spirit. If you can imagine twenty [181] bears dancing to the music of the rattle, whistle, and drum, making odd gambols, and yelling out the most frightful noises, you will have some notion of the bear dance.

Brian. Now for the war dance: that is come at last.

Hunter. It is hardly possible to conceive a more exciting spectacle than that of the war dance among the Sioux. It exhibits Indian manners on the approach of war. As, among civilized people, soldiers are raised either by recruiting or other means; so, among the Indians, something like recruiting prevails. The red pipe is sent through the tribe, and every one who draws a whiff up the stem thereby declares he is willing to join the war party. The warriors then assemble together, painted with vermilion and other colours, and dressed in their war clothes, with their weapons and their war-eagle head-dresses.

Austin. What a sight that must be!

Hunter. When the mystery man has stuck up a red post in the ground, and begun to beat his drum, the warriors advance, one after another, brandishing their war-clubs, and striking the red post a violent blow, while the mystery man sings their death-song. When the warriors have struck the post, they blacken their faces, and all set to dancing around it. The shrill war-whoop is screamed aloud, and frantic gestures and frightful yells show, but too plainly, that there will be very little mercy extended to the enemy that falls into their hands.

Brian. That war dance would make me tremble. [182]

Hunter. The Mandan boys used to assemble at the back of their village, every morning, as soon as the sun was in the skies, to practise sham fighting. Under the guidance and direction of their ablest and most courageous braves and warriors, they were instructed in all the mysteries of war. The preparations, the ambush, the surprise, the combat and the retreat, were made familiar to them. Thus were they bred up from their youth to delight in warfare, and to long for opportunities of using their tomahawks and scalping-knives against their foes.

When you next come to see me, I will give you an account of the cruel customs of the mystery lodge of the Mandans; with the hope that it will increase your abhorrence of cruelty and bloodshed, render you more than ever thankful for the blessings of peace, and more anxious to extend them all over the earth. The hardest of all lessons now, to a red man, is, as I have before intimated, to forgive his enemies; but when, through Divine mercy, his knowledge is extended, and his heart opened to receive the truths of the gospel, he will be enabled to understand, to love, and to practise the injunction of the Saviour, "Love your enemies, bless them that curse you, do good to them that hate you, and pray for them which despitefully use you, and persecute you."

Interior of a Mystery Lodge.

CHAPTER XIII. [183]

It was well for Austin Edwards and his brothers, that their acquaintance with their friend the hunter commenced during one of their holidays, so that they were enabled to pay him a visit more frequently than they otherwise could have done. The life led by the hunter would have been far too solitary for most people; but his long wanderings in the extended prairies, and his long sojournings in places remote from society, had rendered the quiet tranquillity of country scenes pleasant to him: yet, still, as variety has its charms, it afforded him a pleasant change, whenever the three brothers visited him.

In his younger days, he had entered on the life of a hunter and trapper with much ardour. To [184] pursue the buffalo (or, more properly speaking, the bison) of the prairie, the deer, and other animals, and to mingle with the different tribes of Indians, was his delight. With wild animals and wild men he became familiar, and even the very dangers that beset his path gave an interest to his pursuits: but his youth was gone, his manhood was declining, and the world that he once looked upon as an abiding dwelling-place, he now regarded as the pathway to a better home.

Time was, when to urge the arrow or the spear into the heart of the flying prey for mere diversion, and to join in the wild war-whoop of contending tribes, was congenial to his spirit; but his mind had been sobered, so that now to practise forbearance and kindness was far more pleasant than to indulge in cruelty and revenge. He looked on mankind as one great family, which ought to dwell in brotherly love; and he regarded the animal creation as given by a heavenly Hand, for the use, and not the abuse, of man.

In relating the scenes in which he had mingled in earlier years, he was aware that he could not avoid calling up, in some measure, in the youthful hearts of his auditors, the natural desire to see what was new and strange and wonderful, without reflecting a moment on the good or the evil of the thing set before them: but he endeavoured to blend with his descriptions such remarks as would lead them to love what was right and to hate what was wrong. Regarding the Indian tribes as an injured people, he sought to set before his young friends the wrongs and oppressions [185] practised on the red man; that they might sympathize with his trials, and feel interested for his welfare.

The few words that had dropped from his lips, about the ordeal through which the Indians pass before they are allowed to join war-parties, had awakened Austin's curiosity. Nor was it long before, seated with his brothers in the cottage, he was listening to the whole account. "Please to begin at the very beginning," said he, "and I shall not lose a single word."

Hunter. The Sioux, the Crows, the Sacs, the Ojibbeways, the Camanchees, and the Chippewas, all exhibit astonishing proofs of patience and endurance under pain; but in none of the tribes has ever such torture been inflicted, or such courage witnessed, in enduring torment, as among the Mandans.

Brian. Now we shall hear.

Hunter. The Mandans, who, as I have already told you, lived, when I was a hunter, on the Upper Missouri, held a mystery lodge every year; and this was indeed a very solemn gathering of the tribe. I was never present in the lodge on this occasion, but will give you the description of an eye-witness.

Basil. Why did they get together? What did they do?

Hunter. You shall hear. The mystery lodge, or it may be called the religious meeting, was held, first, to appease the wrath and secure the protection of the good and the evil spirits; secondly, to celebrate the great flood, which they [186] believed took place a long time ago; thirdly, to perform the buffalo dance, to bring buffaloes; and, fourthly, to try the strength, courage and endurance of their young men, that they might know who were the most worthy among them, and the most to be relied on in war-parties.

Austin. How came the Mandans to know any thing about the flood, if they have no Bibles?

Hunter. That I cannot tell. Certain it is, that they had a large, high tub, called the Great Canoe, in the centre of their village, set up in commemoration of the flood; and that they held the mystery lodge when the willow leaves were in their prime under the river bank, because, they said, a bird had brought a willow bough in full leaf to the Great Canoe in the flood.

Austin. Why, it is just as if they had read the Bible.

Hunter. The fact of the deluge (however they came by it) had undoubtedly been handed down among them by tradition for many generations: but I must go on with my account of the Mandan gathering. The mystery lodge was opened by a strange-looking man, whom no one seemed to know, and who came from the prairie. This odd man called for some edge-tool at every wigwam in the village; and all these tools, at the end of the ceremonies, were cast into the river from a high bank; as an offering, I suppose, to the Water spirit. After opening the mystery lodge, and appointing a medicine man to preside, he once more disappeared on the prairie.

Brian. What an odd thing! [187]

Hunter. Twenty or thirty young men were in the lodge, candidates for reputation among the tribe, who had presented themselves to undergo the prescribed tortures. As they reclined in the lodge, every one had hung up over his head, his shield, his bow and quiver, and his medicine bag. The young men were painted different colours. The old mystery man appointed to superintend the ceremonies sat by a fire in the middle of the lodge, smoking leisurely with his medicine pipe, in honour of the Great Spirit; and there he sat for four days, and as many nights, during which the young men neither tasted food nor drink, nor were they allowed to close their eyes.

Basil. It was enough to kill them all.

Hunter. On the floor of the lodge were buffalo and human skulls, and sacks filled with water, shaped like tortoises, with sticks by them. During each of the four days, the buffalo dance was performed over and over again, by Indians, painted, and wearing over them whole buffalo skins, with tails and hoofs and horns; while in their hands they carried rattles, and long, thin, white wands, and bore on their backs bundles of green boughs of the willow. Some of the dancers were painted red, to represent the day; and others black, with stars, to resemble the night. During these dances, which took place round the Great Canoe, the tops of the wigwams were crowded with people.

Austin. I want to hear about the young Indians in the lodge, and that old fellow, the mystery man.

Hunter. The superstitious and cruel practices [188] of the mystery lodge are too fearful to dwell upon. I shall only just glance at them, that you may know, in some degree, the kind of trials the young Indians have to endure. While the dances were going on, mystery men, inside the lodge, were beating on the water sacks with sticks, and animating the young men to act courageously, telling them that the Great Spirit was sure to support them. Splints, or wooden skewers, were then run through the flesh on the back and breasts of the young warriors, and they were hoisted up, with cords fastened to the splints, towards the top of the lodge. Not a muscle of their features expressed fear or pain.

Basil. Shocking! shocking!

Brian. That must be horrible!

Hunter. After this, other splints were run through their arms, thighs and legs; and on these were hung their shields, arms and medicine bags. In this situation they were taunted, and turned round with poles till they fainted; and when, on being let down again, they recovered, those who had superior hardihood would crawl to the buffalo skull in the centre of the lodge, and lay upon it the little finger of their left hand to be chopped off; and even the loss of a second or third finger is counted evidence of superior boldness and devotion. After this, they were hurried along between strong and fleet runners: this was called "the last race," round and round the Great Canoe, till the weight of their arms having pulled the splints from their bodies, they once more fainted, and in this state, apparently dead, they [189] were left to themselves, to live or die, as the Great Spirit might determine.

Austin. I should think that hardly any of them would ever come to life again.

Hunter. Nor would they, under common circumstances; but, when we consider that these young men had fasted for four days, and lost much blood in their tortures, there was not much danger of inflammation from their wounds, and their naturally strong constitutions enabled them to recover. All these tortures were willingly undertaken; nor would any one of those who endured them, on any account whatever, have evaded them. To propitiate the Great Spirit, and to stand well in the estimation of his own tribe, are the two highest objects in the mind of an Indian.

The day after that on which Austin and his brothers heard from the hunter the account of the mystery lodge, and the sufferings of the young Mandans before they were thought equal to engage in a war-party, two or three little accidents occurred. In the first place, Austin, in making a new bow, cut a deep gash in his finger: and, in the next, Brian and Basil, in scrambling among the hedges in quest of straight twigs for arrows, met with their mishaps; for Brian got a thorn in his thumb, while Basil had a roll down the bank into a dry ditch.

It is always a good sign in young people, when they put into practice any real or supposed good quality of which they hear or read. The patience [190] and endurance of the young Mandans had called forth high commendations from Austin, and it was evident, in the affair of the cut finger, that he made a struggle, and a successful one too, in controlling his feelings. With an air of resolution, he wrapped the end of his pocket handkerchief tightly round the wound, and passed off the occurrence as a matter of no moment. Not a word escaped little Basil when he rolled into the ditch; nor did Brian utter a single "oh!" when the thorn was extracted from his thumb.

A War-Party.

"You may depend upon it," said Austin, after some conversation with Brian and Basil, on the subject of the young Mandans, "that the next time we see the hunter, we shall hear something about the way in which red men go to war. The sham fight, and the preparation of the young warriors, will be followed by some account of their [191] battles." In this supposition he was quite correct; for, when they next visited the cottage, the hunter proposed to speak a little about councils and encampments and alarms and surprises and attacks. The conversation was carried on in the following manner.

Austin. How do the Indians poison their arrows?

Hunter. By dipping the point of the arrow-head into the poison prepared. The head of the arrow, as I told you, is put on very slightly, so that it remains in the wound when the arrow is withdrawn.

Brian. Where do they get their poison? What is it made of?

Hunter. No doubt there is some difference in the manner of preparing poison among the different tribes. But, usually, it is, I believe, composed of deadly vegetable substances, slowly boiled together, sometimes mingled with the mortal poison of snakes and

148

ants. This is prepared with great care. Its strength is usually tried on a lizard, or some other cold-blooded, slow-dying animal. It is rapid in its effects; for, if a fowl be wounded with a poisoned weapon, it dies in a few minutes; a cat dies in five minutes; a bison, in five or six; and a horse, in ten. Jaguars and deer live but a short time after they are thus wounded. If, then, horses and bisons are so soon destroyed by the poison, no wonder that men should be unable to endure its fatal effects.

Before war is determined on among the Indians, a council is held with great solemnity. The [192] chiefs, and braves, and medicine men are assembled. Then the enlisting takes place, which I have already described; the war dance is engaged in, and weapons are examined and repaired. The chief, arrayed in full dress, leads on his band. They march with silence and rapidity, and encamp with great caution, appointing sentinels in every necessary direction. Thus, lurking, skulking and marching, they reach the place of their destination. Another war council is held, to decide on the mode of attack; and then, with rifles, war-clubs, scalping-knives and bows and poisoned arrows, they fall upon their unsuspecting foes.

Brian. It is very sad to fight with such weapons as poisoned arrows.

Hunter. It is sad to fight with any kind of weapons; but, when once anger enters the heart, and the desire to shed blood is called forth, no mode is thought too cruel that will assist in obtaining a victory. The continual warfare that is carried on between Indian tribes must be afflictive to every humane and Christian spirit. None but the God of peace can destroy the love of war in the hearts of either red or white men.

Indians fight in a way very different from civilized people; for they depend more on cunning, stratagem and surprise, than on skill and courage. Almost all their attacks are made under cover of night, or when least expected. A war-party will frequently go a great distance, to fall upon a village or an encampment on a quarter most accessible. To effect their object, they will hide for any length of time in the forest, sleep in the long [193] grass, lurk in the ravine, and skulk at nightfall around the place to be attacked.

Austin. Did you ever go out with the Indians to fight?

Hunter. Yes. For some time I was treated very hospitably among the Crows, near the Rocky Mountains; and as they had determined to go on one of their war-parties, which I could not prevent, I resolved to go along with them, to watch their way of proceeding.

Austin. Do tell us all about it.

Hunter. It was a thoughtless and foolish affair, when I was young and rash; but I wished to be a spectator of all their customs. It was, as I said, one of those foolish undertakings into which the ardour of my disposition led me, and for which I was very near paying the price of my life. A council was held, wherein it was decided to send a strong war-party on foot to surprise a Blackfoot village. Every stratagem had been used to lull the enemy into security.

Brian. Ay; that is just like the Indians.

Hunter. The red pipe was sent through the tribe, for the warriors to smoke with it, much after the manner of the Sioux; the red post was struck, and the braves and attendants painted their faces. When the plan of attack was agreed on, every warrior looked to his weapons; neither bow nor arrow, war-club nor scalping-knife, was left unexamined. There was an earnestness in their preparation, as though they were all animated with one spirit.

It was some time after sundown, that we left [194] the village at a quick pace. Runners were sent out in all directions, to give notice of an enemy. We hastened along a deep valley, rounded the base of a bluff, and entered the skirt of a forest, following each other in files beneath the shadowy branches. We then passed through some deep grass, and stole silently along several defiles and ravines. The nearer we drew to the Blackfoot village, the more silently and stealthily we proceeded. Like the panther, creeping with noiseless feet on his prey, we stole along the intricate pathways of the prairie bottoms, the forest, the skirt of the river and the hills and bluffs. At last we made a halt, just as the moon emerged from behind a cloud.

Austin. Then there was terrible work, I dare say.

Hunter. It was past midnight, and the Blackfoot village was wrapped in slumber. The Crow warriors dispersed themselves to attack the village at the same instant from different quarters. The leader had on his full dress, his medicine bag, and his head-dress of war-eagle plumes. All was hushed in silence, nearly equal to that of the grave; when suddenly the shrill war-whistle of the Crow chief rung through the Blackfoot lodges, and the wild war-whoop burst at once from a hundred throats. The chief was in the thickest of the fight. There was no pity for youth or age; the war-club spared not, and the tomahawk was merciless. Yelling like fiends, the Crow warriors fled from hut to hut, from victim to victim. Neither women nor children were spared.

Brian. Dreadful! dreadful! [195]

Hunter. Though taken thus by surprise, the Blackfoot braves, in a little time, began to collect together, clutching their weapons firmly, and rushing on their enemies, determined to avenge their slaughtered friends. The panic into which they had been thrown subsided, and, like men accustomed to danger, they stood not only in self-defence, but attacked their foes with fury.

Austin. I wonder that every one in the Blackfoot village was not killed!

Hunter. In civilized life, this would very likely have been the case; but in a savage state, men from their childhood are trained up to peril. They may lie down to slumber on their couches of skins, but their weapons are near at hand; and though it be the midnight hour when an attack is made on them, and though, awakened by the confusion, they hear nothing but the war-cry of their enemy, they spring to their feet, seize their arms, and rush on to meet their foes. It was thus with the Blackfoot braves. Hand to hand, and foot to foot, they met their assailants; brave was opposed to brave; and the horrid clash of the war-club and the murderous death-grapple succeeded each other. Even if I could describe the horrors of such a scene, it would not be right to do so. As I was gazing on the conflict, I suddenly received a blow that struck me bleeding to the ground. You may see the scar on my temple still. The confusion was at its height, or else my scalp would have been taken.

Brian. How did you get away?

Hunter. Stunned as I was, I recovered my senses before a retreat took place, and was just [196] able to effect my escape. The Crows slaughtered many of their enemies; but the Blackfoot warriors and braves were at last too strong for them. Then was heard the shrill whistle that sounded a retreat. With a dozen scalps in their possession, the Crows sought the shelter of the forest, and afterwards regained their own village.

Austin. Are the Crow tribe or the Blackfoot tribe the strongest?

Hunter. The Crow Indians, as I told you, are taller and more elegant men than the Blackfeet; but the latter have broader chests and shoulders. The Blackfeet, some think, take their name from the circumstance of their wearing black, or very dark brown leggings and mocassins. Whether, as a people, the Crows or the Blackfeet are the strongest, there is a diversity of opinion. The Blackfeet are almost always at war with the Crows.

Austin. What battling there must be among them!

Hunter. Their war-parties are very numerous, and their encampments are very large: and, whether seen in the day, in the midst of their lodges; or at night, wrapped in their robes, with their arms in their hands, ready to leap up if attacked by an enemy; they form a striking spectacle. Sometimes, in a night encampment, a false alarm takes place. A prowling bear, or a stray horse, is taken for a foe; and sometimes a real alarm is occasioned by spies crawling on their hands and knees up to their very encampment to ascertain their strength. On these occasions the shrill [197] whistle is heard, every man springs up armed and rushes forth, ready to resist his assailing enemy. I have seen war-parties among the Crows and Blackfeet, the Mandans and Sioux, the Shawanees, Poncas, Pawnees and Seminoles. But a Camanchee war-party, mounted on wild horses, with their shields, bows and lances, which I once witnessed, was the most imposing spectacle of the kind I ever saw. The chief was mounted on a beautiful war-horse, wild as the winds, and yet he appeared to manage him with ease. He was in full dress, and seemed to have as much fire in his disposition as the chafed animal on which he rode. In his bridle-hand, he clutched his bow and several arrows; with his other hand, he wielded his long lance; while his quiver and shield were slung at his back, and his rifle across his thigh.

Austin. I think I can see him. But what colour was his war-horse?

152

Hunter. Black as a raven; but the white foam lay in thick flakes on his neck and breast, for his rider at every few paces stuck the sharp rowels of his Spanish spurs into his sides. He had a long flowing mane and tail, and his full and fiery eyes seemed ready to start out of his head. The whole Camanchee band was ready to rush into any danger. At one time, they were flying over the prairie in single file; and at another, drawn up all abreast of each other. The Camanchees and the Osages used to have cruel battles one with another. The Mandans and the Riccarees, too, were relentless enemies. [198]

Brian. And the Sacs and Foxes were great fighters, for Black Hawk was a famous fellow.

Hunter. Yes, he was. But I have never told you, I believe, how the medicine man, or mystery man, conducts himself when called unto a wounded warrior.

Austin. Not a word of it. Please to tell us every particular.

Hunter. In some cases cures are certainly performed; in others, the wounded get well of themselves: but, in most instances, the mystery man is a mere juggler.

Basil. Now we shall hear of the mystery man.

Hunter. The Crow war-party that I had joined brought away two of their wounded warriors when they retreated from the Blackfoot village, but there seemed to be no hope of saving their lives. However, a mystery man was called on to use his skill.

Austin. Ay; I want to know how the mystery man cures his patients.

Hunter. If ever you should require a doctor, I hope you will have one more skilful than the mystery man that I am going to describe. The wounded warriors were in extremity, and I thought that one of them was dying before the mystery man made his appearance; but you shall hear. The wounded men lay groaning on the ground, with Indians around them, who kept moaning even louder than they did; when, all at once, a scuffle of feet and a noise like that of a low rattle were heard. [199]

Austin. The mystery man was coming, I suppose.

Hunter. He was; and a death-like silence was instantly preserved by all the attendant Indians. In came the mystery man, covered over with the shaggy hide of a yellow bear, so that, had it not been that his mocassins, leggings and hands were visible, you might have supposed a real bear was walking upright, with a spear in one paw, and a rattle, formed like a tambourine, in the other.

Basil. He could never cure the dying man with his tambourine.

Hunter. From the yellow bear-skin hung a profusion of smaller skins, such as those of different kinds of snakes, toads, frogs and bats; with hoofs of animals, beaks and tails of birds, and scraps and fragments of other things; a complete bundle of odds and ends. The medicine man came into the circle, bending his knees, crouching, sliding one foot after the other along the ground, and now and then leaping and grunting. You could not see his face, for the yellow bear-head skin covered it, and the paws dangled before him. He shuffled round and round the wounded men, shaking his rattle and making all kinds of odd noises; he then stopped to turn them over.

Austin. He had need of all his medicine.

Hunter. Hardly had he been present a minute, before one of the men died; and, in ten minutes more, his companion breathed his last. The medicine man turned them over, shook his rattle over them, howled, groaned and grunted; but it would not do; the men were dead, and all his mummery [200] would not bring them back to life again; so, after a few antics of various kinds, he shuffled off with himself, shaking his rattle, and howling and groaning louder than ever. You may remember, that I told you of the death of Oseola, the Seminole chief: he who struck his dagger through the treaty that was to sign away the hunting-grounds of his tribe, in exchange for distant lands.

Austin. Yes. You said that he dashed his dagger not only through the contract, but also through the table on which it lay.

Brian. And you told us that he was taken prisoner by treachery and died in captivity.

Hunter. Now I will tell you the particulars of his death; for I only said before, that he died pillowed on the faithful bosom of his wife.

He had his two wives with him when he died, but one was his favourite.

Austin. Please to let us know every thing about him. It was at Fort Moultrie in Charleston, South Carolina.

Hunter. Finding himself at the point of death, he made signs that the chiefs and officers might be assembled, and his wishes were immediately complied with. The next thing he desired was, that his war-dress, that dress in which he had so often led his tribe to victory, might be brought to him. His wife waited obediently upon him, and his war-dress was placed before him.

Basil. What could he want of his war-dress when he was going to die?

Austin. Wait a little, Basil, and you will hear all about it, I dare say. [201]

Hunter. It was an affecting sight, to see him get up from his bed on the floor, once more to dress himself as a chief of his tribe, just as if he was about to head an expedition against the whites. Well, he put on his rich mocassins, his leggings adorned with scalp-locks, his shirt and his ornamental belt of war. Nor did he forget the pouch that carried his bullets, the horn that held his powder; nor the knife with which he had taken so many scalps.

Brian. How very strange for a dying man to dress himself in that way!

Hunter. In all this, he was as calm and as steady as though about to hunt in the woods with his tribe. He then made signs, while sitting up in his bed, that his red paint should be given him, and his looking-glass held up, that he might paint his face.

Austin. And did he paint his face himself?

Hunter. Only one half of it; after which his throat, neck, wrists and the backs of his hands were made as red as vermilion would make them. The very handle of his knife was coloured over in the same way.

Basil. What did he paint his hands and his knife-handle for?

Hunter. Because it was the custom of his tribe, and of his fathers before him, to paint themselves and their weapons red, whenever they took an oath of destruction to their enemies. Oseola did it, no doubt, that he might die like a chief of his tribe; that he might show those around him, that, even in death, he did not forget that he was a [202] Seminole warrior. In that awful hour, he put on his splendid turban with its three ostrich feathers, and then, being wearied with the effort he had made, he lay down to recover his strength.

Austin. How weak he must have been!

Hunter. In a short time he rose again, sitting in his full dress like the leader of a warlike tribe, and calmly and smilingly extended his hand to the chiefs and officers, to his wives and his children. But this, his last effort, exhausted his remaining strength. He was lowered down on the bed, calmly drew his scalping-knife from its sheath under his war-belt, where it had been placed, and grasped it with firmness and dignity. With his hands crossed on his manly breast, and with a smile on his face, he breathed his last. Thus passed away the spirit of Oseola.

Austin. Poor Oseola! He died like a chief, at last.

Hunter. He did, but not like a Christian, and, very likely, when he grasped his scalping-knife, before his last breath forsook him, some glowing vision of successful combat was before him. In the pride of his heart, perhaps, he was leading on his braves to mingle in the clash of battle and the death-grapple with his enemies. But is this a fit state of mind for a man to die in? Much as we may admire the steady firmness and unsubdued courage of an Indian warrior in death, emotions of pride and high-mindedness, and thoughts of bloodshed and victory, are as far removed as possible from the principles of Christianity, and most [203] unsuitable to a dying hour. Humility, forgiveness, repentance, hope, faith, peace and joy, are needed at such a season; and the time will come, we trust, when Indians, taught better by the gospel, will think and feel so.

Mounted Chief.

CHAPTER XIV. [204]

The holidays of the three brothers were drawing to a close; and this circumstance rendered them the more anxious to secure one or two more visits to the cottage, before they settled down in right earnest to their books. Brian and Basil talked much about the poisoned arrows, and the mystery man; but Austin's mind was too much occupied with the Camanchee chief on his black war-horse, and the death of the Seminole chief Oseola, to think much of any thing else. He thought there was something very noble in the [205] valour of a chief leading on his tribe to conquest; and something almost sublime in a warrior dressing himself up in his war-robes to die. Like many other young people of ardent dispositions, he seemed to forget, that when a victory is enjoyed, a defeat must be endured; and that before any one can rejoice in taking a scalp, some one must be rendered miserable or lifeless by losing it. The remarks of the hunter, respecting the inconsistency of such customs with the peaceful principles of religion, especially the solemnities of a dying hour, had not been made altogether in vain; yet still he dwelt on the image of Oseola grasping his scalping-knife, crossing his hands over his breast, and dying with a smile on his countenance.

On their next walk to the cottage, the way was beguiled by endeavouring to call to mind all that had been told them on their last visit; and, to do him justice, he acquitted himself uncommonly well. It is true, that now and then his brothers refreshed his memory on some points which had escaped him; but, on the whole, his account was full, connected, and clear.

"And what must I tell you now?" said the hunter, as soon as he and the young people had exchanged salutations. "Do you not know enough about the Indians?"

To this inquiry, Brian replied that what they had heard had only increased their curiosity to hear more.

"Well; let me consider," said the hunter. "I have told you about the different tribes of Indians, [206] their religion, languages, manners and customs; their villages, wigwams, food, dress, arms and musical instruments. I have described to you the fur trade; and dwelt on the scenery of the country, the mountains, rivers, lakes, prairies and many remarkable places. I have related the adventures of Black Hawk and Nikkanochee. And, besides these things, you have had a tolerably full account of buffaloes, bears, wild horses, wolves, deer and other animals, with the manner of hunting them; as well as a relation of Indian amusements, dances, sham fights, war-parties, encampments, alarms, attacks, scalping and retreats. Let me now, then, dwell a little on the Indian way of concluding a treaty of peace, and on a few other matters; after which, I will conclude with the best account I can give you of what the missionaries have done among the different tribes."

Austin. I shall be very sorry when you have told us all.

Brian. And so shall I: for it is so pleasing to come here, and listen to what you tell us.

Hunter. When it is agreed between hostile tribes that a treaty of peace shall be made, the chiefs and medicine men of the adverse tribes meet together, and the calumet, or peace-pipe, ornamented with eagle quills, being produced, every one smokes a few whiffs through it. It is then understood by them that the tomahawk is to be buried. The pipe-of-peace dance is then performed by the warriors, to the beat of the Indian drum and rattle, every warrior holding his pipe in his hand. [207]

Brian. That pipe-of-peace dance is a capital dance, for then bloodshed is at an end.

Hunter. Unfortunately, war is apt soon to break out again, and then the buried tomahawk becomes as busy as ever.

Austin. Well, I do like the Indians, in spite of all their faults, and I think they have been used cruelly by the whites.

Hunter. As a general remark, those Indians who have had least to do with civilized life are the most worthy of regard. Such as live near white men, or such as are frequently visited by them, seem to learn quickly the vices of others, without giving up their own. To observe the real character of red men, it is necessary to trace the turnings and windings of the Yellow Stone River, or the yet more remote sinuosities of the Upper Missouri. The nearer the United

States, the more servile is the Indian character; and the nearer the Rocky Mountains, the more independent and open-hearted.

Austin. If I ever go among the red men, the Yellow Stone River, or the Upper Missouri, will be the place for me.

Hunter. Many of the chiefs of the tribes near the Rocky Mountains may be said to live in a state of splendour. They have the pure air of heaven around them and rivers abounding in fish. The prairie yields them buffaloes in plenty; and, as for their lodges and dress, some of them may be called sumptuous. Sometimes, twenty or thirty buffalo skins, beautifully dressed, are joined together to form a covering for a lodge; and their [208] robes and different articles of apparel are so rich with ermine, the nails and claws of birds and animals, war-eagle plumes, and embroidery of highly coloured porcupine quills, that a monarch in his coronation robes is scarcely a spectacle more imposing.

Austin. Ay, I remember the dress of Mah-to-toh-pa, "the four bears," his buffalo robe, his porcupine-quilled leggings, his embroidered buckskin mocassins, his otter necklace, his buffalo horns, and his splendid head-dress of war-eagle plumes.

Hunter. In a state of war, it is the delight of a chief to leap on the back of his fiery steed, decorated as the leader of his tribe, and armed with his glittering lance and unerring bow, to lead on his band to victory. In the chase, he is as ardent as in the battle; smiling at danger, he plunges, on his flying steed, among a thousand buffaloes, launching his fatal shafts with deadly effect. Thus has the Indian of the far-west lived, and thus is he living still. But the trader and the rum-bottle, and the rifle and the white man are on his track; and, like his red brethren who once dwelt east of the Mississippi, he must fall back yet farther, and gradually decline before the approach of civilization.

Austin. It is a very strange thing that white men will not let red men alone. What right have they to cheat them of their hunting-grounds?

Hunter. I will relate to you an account, that appeared some time ago in most of the newspapers (though I cannot vouch for the truth of it,) of a chief who, though he was respected by his [209] tribe before he went among the whites, had very little respect paid to him afterwards.

Brian. I hope it is a long account.

Hunter. Not very long: but you shall hear. "In order to assist the officers of the Indian department, in their arduous duty of persuading remote tribes to quit their lands, it has been found advisable to incur the expense of inviting one or two of their chiefs some two or three thousand miles to Washington, in order that they should see with their own eyes, and report to their tribes, the irresistible power of the nation with which they are arguing. This speculation has, it is said, in all instances, more or less effected its object. For the reasons and for the objects we have stated, it was deemed advisable that a certain chief should be invited from his remote country to Washington; and accordingly, in due time, he appeared there."

Austin. Two or three thousand miles! What a distance for him to go!

Hunter. "After the troops had been made to manœuvre before him; after thundering volleys of artillery had almost deafened him; and after every department had displayed to him all that was likely to add to the terror and astonishment he had already experienced, the President, in lieu of the Indian's clothes, presented him with a colonel's uniform; in which, and with many other presents, the bewildered chief took his departure."

Brian. He would hardly know how to walk in a colonel's uniform.

Hunter. "In a pair of white kid gloves; tight blue coat, with gilt buttons, gold epaulettes, and [210] red sash; cloth trowsers with straps; high-heeled boots; cocked hat, and scarlet feather; with a cigar in his mouth, a green umbrella in one hand, and a yellow fan in the other; and with the neck of a whiskey bottle protruding out of each of the two tail-pockets of his regimental coat; this 'monkey that had seen the world' suddenly appeared before the chiefs and warriors of his tribe; and as he stood before them, straight as a ramrod, in a high state of perspiration, caused by the tightness of his finery, while the cool fresh air of heaven blew over the naked, unrestrained limbs of the spectators, it might, perhaps not unjustly, be said of the costumes, 'Which is the savage?' In return for the presents he had received, and with a desire to impart as much real information as possible to his tribe, the poor jaded traveller undertook to deliver to them a course of lectures, in which he graphically described all that he had witnessed."

Austin. An Indian in white kid gloves, blue coat, high-heeled boots, and cocked hat and feather! Why his tribe would all laugh at him, in spite of his lectures.

Hunter. "For a while he was listened to with attention; but as soon as the minds of his audience had received as much as they could hold, they began to disbelieve him. Nothing daunted, however, the traveller still proceeded."

Austin. I thought they would laugh at him.

Hunter. "He told them about wigwams, in which a thousand people could at one time pray to the Great Spirit; of other wigwams, five stories [211] high, built in lines, facing each other, and extending over an enormous space: he told them of war canoes that would hold twelve hundred warriors."

Austin. They would be sure never to believe him.

Hunter. "Such tales, to the Indian mind, seemed an insult to common sense. For some time he was treated merely with ridicule and contempt; but, when, resolutely continuing to recount his adventures, he told them about a balloon, and that he had seen white people, who, by attaching a great ball to a canoe, as he described it, could rise in it up to the clouds, and travel through the heavens, the medicine, or mystery men of his tribe pronounced him to be an impostor; and the multitude vociferously declaring that he was too great a liar to live, a young warrior, in a paroxysm of anger, levelled a rifle and shot him dead!"

Austin. Well, I am very sorry! It was very silly to be dressed up in that way; but they ought not to have killed him, for he told them the truth, after all.

Brian. I could never have thought that an Indian chief would have dressed himself in a blue coat and gilt buttons.

Basil. And, then, the fan and green umbrella!

Austin. Ay, and the whiskey bottles sticking out of his tail-pockets. He would look a little different from Mah-to-toh-pa.

Hunter. I have frequently spoken of the splendid head-dress of the chiefs of some tribes. Among the Mandans, (and you know Mah-to-toh-pa was [212] a Mandan,) they would not part with one of their head-dresses of war-eagle plumes at a less price than two horses. The Konzas, Osages, Pawnees, Sacs, Foxes and Iowas shave their heads; but all the rest, or at least as far as I know of the Indian tribes, wear long hair.

Brian. Yes; we remember the Crows, with their hair sweeping the ground.

Hunter. Did I tell you, that some of the tribes glue other hair to their own to make it long, as it is considered so ornamental?

Basil. I do not remember that you told us that.

Hunter. There are a few other things respecting the Indians that I wish to mention, before I tell you what the missionaries have done among them. In civilized countries, people turn out their toes in walking; but this is not the case among the Indians. When the toes are turned out, either in walking or running, the whole weight of the body falls too much on the great toe of the foot that is behind, and it is mainly owing to this circumstance, that so many have a deformity at the joint of the great toe. When the foot is turned in, the weight of the body is thrown equally on all the toes, and the deformity of the great toe joint is avoided.

Austin. What! do the Indians know better how to walk than we do? If theirs is the best way to walk, why do not we all walk so?

Hunter. I suppose, because it is not so elegant in appearance to walk so. But many things are done by civilized people on account of fashion. Hundreds and hundreds of females shorten their [213] lives by the tight clothing and lacings with which they compress their bodies; but the Indians do not commit such folly.

Brian. There is something to be learned from the Indians, after all.

Hunter. There is a custom among the Sacs and Foxes that I do not think I spoke of. The Sacs are better provided with horses than the Foxes: and so, when the latter go to war and want horses, they go to the Sacs and beg them. After a time, they sit round in a circle, and take up their pipes to smoke, seemingly quite at their ease; and, while they are whiffing away, the young men of the Sacs ride round and round the circle, every now and then cutting at the shoulders of the Foxes with their whips, making the blood start forth. After keeping up this strange custom for some time, the young Sacs dismount, and present their horses to those they have been flogging.

Austin. What a curious custom! I should not much like to be flogged in that manner.

Hunter. There is a certain rock which the Camanchees always visit when they go to war. Putting their horses at full speed, they shoot their best arrows at this rock, which they consider great medicine. If they did not go through this long-established custom, there would be no confidence among them; but, when they have thus sacrificed their best arrows to the rock, their hope and confidence are strong.

Austin. I should have thought they would have wanted their best arrows to fight with. [214]

Hunter. There is no accounting for the superstitions of people. There is nothing too absurd to gain belief even among civilized nations, when they give up the truth of God's word, and follow the traditions or commandments of men. The Sioux have a strange notion about thunder; they say that the thunder is hatched by a small bird, not much bigger than the humming-bird. There is, in the Couteau des Prairies, a place called "the nest of the thunder;" and, in the small bushes there, they will have it that this little bird sits upon its eggs till the long claps of thunder come forth. Strange as this tradition is, there would be no use in denying it; for the superstition of the Indian is too strong to be easily done away with. The same people, before they go on a buffalo hunt, usually pay a visit to a spot where the form of a buffalo is cut out on a prairie. This figure is great medicine; and the hunt is sure to be more prosperous, in their opinion, after it has been visited.

Austin. I do hope that we shall forget none of these curious things.

Eliot Preaching to the Indians.

CHAPTER XV. [215]

For the last time but one, during their holidays, Austin and his brothers set off, with a long afternoon before them, to listen to the hunter's account of the proceedings of the missionaries among the Indians. On this occasion, they paid another visit to the Red Sandstone Rock by the river, the place where they first met with their friend, the hunter. Here they recalled to mind all the circumstances which had taken place at that spot, and agreed that the hunter, in saving their lives by his timely warning, and afterwards adding so much as he had done to their information and pleasure, had been to them one of the best friends they had ever known. With very friendly [216] and grateful feelings towards him, they hastened to the cottage, when the Indians, as usual, became the subject of their conversation. "And now," said Austin, "we are quite ready to hear about the missionaries."

Hunter. Let me speak a word or two about the Indians, before I begin my account. You remember that I told you of the Mandans.

Austin. Yes. Mah-to-toh-pa was a Mandan, with his fine robes and war-eagle head-dress. The rain-makers were Mandans; also the young warriors, who went through so many tortures in the mystery lodge.

Hunter. Well, I must now tell you a sad truth. After I left the Mandans, great changes came upon them; and, at the present time, hardly a single Mandan is alive.

Austin. Dreadful! But how was it? What brought it all about?

Brian. You should have told us this before.

Hunter. No. I preferred to tell you first of the people as they were when I was with them. You may remember my observation, in one of your early visits, that great changes had taken place among them; that the tomahawks of the stronger tribes had thinned the others; that many had sold their lands to the whites, and retired to the west of the Mississippi; and that thousands had fallen a prey to the smallpox. It was in the year 1838 that this dreadful disease was introduced among the Mandans, and other tribes of the fur-traders. Of the Blackfeet, Crows and two or three other tribes, twenty-five thousand perished; [217] but of the poor Mandans, the whole tribe was destroyed.

Brian. Why did they not get a doctor; or go out of their village to the wide prairie, that one might not catch the disease from another?

Hunter. Doctors were too far off; and the ravages of the disease were so swift that it swept them all away in a few months. Their mystery men could not help them; and their enemies, the Sioux, had war-parties round their village, so that they could not go out to the wide prairie. There they were, dying fast in their village; and little else was heard, during day or night, but wailing, howling and crying to the Great Spirit to relieve them.

Austin. And did Mah-to-toh-pa, "the four bears," die too?

Hunter. Yes. For, though he recovered from the disease, he could not bear up against the loss of his wives and his children. They all died before his eyes, and he piled them together in his lodge, and covered them with robes. His braves and his warriors died, and life had no charms for him; for who was to share with him his joy or his grief? He retired from his wigwam, and fasted six days, lamenting the destruction of his tribe. He then crawled back to his own lodge, laid himself by his dead family, covered himself with a robe, and died like an Indian chief. This is a melancholy picture; and when I first heard of the terrible event, I could have wept.

Austin. It was indeed a terrible affair. Have they no good doctors among the Indians now? [218] Why do they not send for doctors who know how to cure the small-pox, instead of those juggling mystery men?

Hunter. Many attempts have been made to introduce vaccination among the tribes; but their jealousy and want of confidence in white men, who have so much wronged them, and their attachment to their own customs and superstitions, have prevented those attempts from being very successful.

Austin. Who was the first missionary who went among the Indians?

Hunter. I believe the first Indian missionary was John Eliot. More than two hundred years ago, a body of pious Englishmen left their native land, because they were not allowed peaceably to serve God according to their consciences. They landed in America, having obtained a grant of land there. They are sometimes called "Puritans," and sometimes "the Pilgrim Fathers." It is certain, that, whatever were their peculiarities, and by whatever names they were known, the fear of God and the love of mankind animated their hearts.

These men did not seize the possessions of the Indians, because they had arms and skill to use them. But they entered into a treaty with them for the purchase of their lands, and paid them what they were satisfied to receive. It is true, that what the white man gave in exchange was of little value to him. But the Indians prized trinkets more than they would gold and silver, [219] and they only wanted hunting and fishing grounds for their own use. These early colonists, seeing that the Indians were living in idleness, cruelty and superstition, were desirous to instruct them in useful arts, and still more in the fear of the Lord; and John Eliot, who had left England to join his religious friends in America, was the first Protestant missionary among the Indians.

Austin. I wonder he was not afraid of going among them.

Hunter. He that truly fears God has no need to fear danger in the path of duty. John Eliot had three good motives that girded his loins and strengthened his heart: the first, was the glory of God, in the conversion of the poor Indians; the second, was his love of mankind, and pity for such as were ignorant of true religion; and the third, was his desire that the promise of his friends to spread the gospel among the Indians should be fulfilled. It was no light task that he had undertaken, as I will prove to you. I dare say, that you have not quite forgotten all the long names that I gave you.

Austin. I remember your telling us of them; and I suppose they are the longest words in the world.

Hunter. I will now give you two words in one of the languages that John Eliot had to learn, and then, perhaps, you will alter your opinion. The first of them is *noorromantammoonkanunonnash*, which means, "our loves;" and the second, or "our questions," is *kummogokdonattoottammoctiteaongannunnonash*. [220]

Austin. Why that last word would reach all across one of our copy-books.

Basil. You had better learn those two words, Austin, to begin with.

Brian. Ay, do, Austin; if you have many such when you go among the red men, you must sit up at night to learn what you have to speak in the day-time.

Austin. No, no; I have settled all that. I mean to have an interpreter with me; one who knows every thing. Please to tell us a little more about Eliot.

Hunter. I will. An author says, speaking of missionaries, "As I hold the highest title on earth to be that of a servant of God, and the most important employment that of making known to sinners the salvation that God has wrought for them, through his Son Jesus Christ; so I cannot but estimate very highly the character of an humble, zealous, conscientious missionary. Men undertake, endure and achieve much when riches and honours and reputation are to be attained; but where is the worldly reputation of him who goes, with his life in his hand, to make known to barbarous lands the glad tidings of salvation? Where are the honours and the money bags of the missionary? In many cases, toil and anxiety, hunger and thirst, reviling and violence, danger and death await him; but where is his earthly reward?" Eliot's labours were incessant; translating not only the commandments, the Lord's prayer and many parts of Scripture into the Indian languages, but also the whole Bible. For days [221] together he travelled from place to place, wet to the skin, wringing the wet from his stockings at night. Sometimes he was treated cruelly by the sachems, (principal chiefs,) sagamores, (lesser chiefs,) and powaws, (conjurers, or mystery men;) but though they thrust him out, and threatened his life, he held on his course, telling them that he was in the service of the Great God, and feared them not. So highly did they think of his services in England, that a book was printed, called "The Day-breaking, if not the Sun-rising of the Gospel with the Indians in New-England;" and another, entitled "The Clear Sunshine of the Gospel breaking forth upon the Indians;" and dedicated to the parliament; in order that assistance and encouragement might be given him. At the close of a grammar, published by him, he wrote the words, "Prayers and pains, through faith in Christ Jesus, will do any thing."

Brian. I should think that he was one of the best of men.

Hunter. He instituted schools, and devoted himself to the Christian course he had undertaken with an humble and ardent spirit, until old age and increasing infirmities rendered him too feeble to do as he had done before. Even then, he catechised the negro slaves in the neighbourhood around him; and took a poor blind boy home to his own house, that he might teach him to commit to memory some of the chapters in the Bible. Among the last expressions that dropped from his lips were the words, "Welcome joy! Pray! pray! pray!" This was in the eighty-sixth year [222] of his age. No wonder he should even now be remembered by us as "the apostle of the Indians."

Basil. I am very glad that you told us about him. What a good old man he must have been when he died!

Hunter. You will find an interesting history of Eliot in your Sunday-school Library, and the Life of Brainerd [5] also, of whom I will tell you a few things. But I advise you to read both books, for such short remarks as I make cannot be distinctly remembered; and the characters of these eminent men you will only understand by reading the history of their lives.

[5] Both these works are published by the American Sunday-school Union.

Austin. We will remember this.

Hunter. There were many good men, after his death, who trod as closely as they could in his steps: but I must not stop to dwell upon them. David Brainerd, however, must not be passed by: he was a truly humble and zealous servant of the Most High. You may judge, in some degree, of his interest in the Indians by the following extract from his diary:

June 26. "In the morning, my desire seemed to rise, and ascend up freely to God. Was busy most of the day in translating prayers into the language of the Delaware Indians; met with great difficulty, because my interpreter was altogether unacquainted with the business. But though I was much discouraged with the extreme difficulty of that work, yet God supported me; and, especially [223] in the evening, gave me sweet refreshment. In prayer my soul was enlarged, and my faith drawn into sensible exercise; was enabled to cry to God for my poor Indians; and though the work of their conversion appeared *impossible with man,* yet *with God* I saw *all things were possible.* My faith was much strengthened, by observing the wonderful assistance God afforded his servants Nehemiah and Ezra, in reforming his people and re-establishing his ancient church. I was much assisted in prayer for my dear Christian friends, and for others whom I apprehended to be Christ-less; but was more especially concerned for the poor heathen, and those of my own charge; was enabled to be instant in prayer for them; and hoped that God would bow the heavens and come down for their salvation. It seemed to me, that there could be no impediment sufficient to obstruct that glorious work, seeing the living God, as I strongly hoped, was engaged for it. I continued in a solemn frame, lifting up my heart to God for assistance and grace, that I might be more mortified to this present world, that my whole soul might be taken up continually in concern for the advancement of Christ's kingdom. Earnestly desired that God would purge me more, that I might be a chosen vessel to bear his name among the heathens. Continued in this frame till I fell asleep."

Brian. Why, he was much such a man as Eliot.

Hunter. Both Eliot and Brainerd did a great deal of good among the Indians. The language [224] of Brainerd was, "Here am I, Lord, send me; send me to the ends of the earth; send me to the rough, the savage pagans of the wilderness; send me from all that is called comfort on earth; send me even to death itself, if it be but in thy service, and to extend thy kingdom."

Brian. I hardly know whether Eliot was the best man, or Brainerd.

Hunter. They were very unlike in one thing; for Eliot lived till he was eighty-six years old; whereas Brainerd died in the thirtieth year of his age. But though so young, it is said of him, by a learned and good man, "The Life and Diary of David Brainerd exhibits a perfect pattern of the qualities which should distinguish the instructor of rude and barbarous tribes; the most invincible patience and self-denial, the profoundest humility, exquisite prudence, indefatigable industry, and such a devotedness to God, or rather such an absorption of the whole soul in zeal for the Divine glory and the salvation of men, as is scarcely to be paralleled since the age of the apostles."

Brian. Then, he was as good a man as Eliot.

Hunter. You will read his life surely, after all you have heard about the Indians, and will be surprised at his great success among them. I will read you an extract from a letter written in those days by some Oneida chiefs, by which you will see that the labours of these good men were not in vain.

"The holy word of Jesus has got place amongst us, and advances. Many have lately forsaken their sins, to appearance, and turned to God. [225] There are some among us who are very stubborn and strong; but Jesus is almighty, and has all strength, and his holy word is very strong, too: therefore we hope it will conquer and succeed more and more. We say no more; only we ask our fathers to pray for us, though they are at a great distance. Perhaps, by-and-by, through the strength and mercy of Jesus, we shall meet in his kingdom above. Farewell.

- Tagawarow, *chief of the Bear tribe.*
- Sughnagearot, *chief of the Wolf tribe.*
- Ojekheta, *chief of the Turtle tribe.*"

Austin. Why, they were all three of them chiefs!

Hunter. The speech made by the chief, Little Turtle, at Baltimore, on his way to see the President of the United States, will interest you. Some Quakers, who saw him, told him that the habit among his tribe of drinking rum prevented them from doing them good.

"Brothers and friends—When your forefathers first met on this island, your red brethren were very numerous; but, since the introduction amongst us of what you call spirituous liquors, and what we think may justly be called poison, our numbers are greatly diminished. It has destroyed a great part of your red brethren.

"My friends and brothers—We plainly perceive that you see the very evil which destroys your red brethren. It is not an evil of our own making. We have not placed it amongst ourselves; it is an evil placed amongst us by the white people; we look to them to remove it out of the country. We [226] tell them, 'Brethren, fetch us useful things: bring us goods that will clothe us, our women, and our children; and not this evil liquor, that destroys our health, that destroys our reason, that destroys our lives.' But all that we can say on this subject is of no service, nor gives relief to your red brethren.

"My friends and brothers—I rejoice to find that you agree in opinion with us, and express an anxiety to be, if possible, of service to us, in removing this great evil out of our country; an evil which has had so much room in it, and has destroyed so many of our lives, that it causes our young men to say, 'We had better be at war with the white people. This liquor, which they introduced into our country, is more to be feared than the gun or tomahawk.' There are more of us dead since the treaty of Greeneville, than we lost by the six years' war before. It is all owing to the introduction of this liquor among us.

"Brothers—When our young men have been out hunting, and are returning home loaded with skins and furs, on their way, if it happens that they come where this whiskey is deposited, the white man who sells it tells them to take a little drink. Some of them will say, 'No; I do not want it.' They go on till they come to another house, where they find more of the same kind of drink. It is there offered again; they refuse; and again the third time: but, finally, the fourth or fifth time, one accepts of it, and takes a drink, and getting one he wants another, and then a third, and fourth, till his senses have left him. [227] After his reason comes back to him, when he gets up and finds where he is, he asks for his peltry. The answer is, 'You have drunk them.' 'Where is my gun?' 'It is gone.' 'Where is my blanket?' 'It is gone.' 'Where is my shirt?' 'You have sold it for whiskey!' Now, brothers, figure to yourselves what condition this man must be in. He has a family at home; a wife and children who stand in need of the profits of his hunting. What must be their wants, when even he himself is without a shirt?"

Austin. There is a great deal of good sense in what Little Turtle said.

Hunter. The war between England and America made sad confusion among the Indians, and the missionaries too; for it was reported that the missionaries were joining the French against the English, so that they and the Indian converts were dreadfully persecuted.

Colonel de Peyster, who was then the English governor at Fort Detroit, suspected the Christian Indians of being partisans of the Americans, and the missionaries of being spies; and he wished the Indians favourable to him to carry them all off. Captain Pipe, a Delaware chief, persuaded the half king of the Hurons to force them away. Persecution went on, till the missionaries, seeing that no other course remained, they being plundered without mercy, and their lives threatened, consented to emigrate. They were thus compelled to quit their pleasant settlement, escorted by a troop of savages headed by an English officer. The half king of the Hurons went with them. [228] But I will read you an account of what took place after they reached Sandusky Creek. "Having arrived at Sandusky Creek, after a journey of upwards of four weeks, the half king of the Hurons and his warriors left them, and marched into their own country, without giving them any particular orders how to proceed. Thus they were abandoned in a wilderness where there was neither game nor provisions of any kind; such was the place to which the barbarians had led them, notwithstanding they had represented it as a perfect paradise. After wandering to and fro for some time, they resolved to spend the winter in Upper Sandusky; and, having pitched on the most convenient spot they could find in this dreary region, they erected small huts of logs and bark, to shelter themselves from the rain and cold. They were now, however, so poor, that they had neither beds nor blankets; for, on the journey, the savages had stolen every thing from them, except only their utensils for manufacturing maple sugar. But nothing distressed them so much as the want of provisions. Some had long spent their all, and now depended on the charity of their neighbours for a morsel to eat. Even the missionaries, who hitherto had uniformly gained a livelihood by the labour of their hands, were now reduced to the necessity of receiving support from the congregation. As their wants were so urgent, Shebosh the missionary, and several of the Christian

Indians, returned, as soon as possible, to their settlements on the Muskingum, to fetch the Indian corn which they had left growing in the fields. [229]

"Scarcely had the congregation begun to settle in Sandusky, when the missionaries were ordered to go and appear before the governor of Fort Detroit. Four of them, accompanied by several of the Indian assistants, accordingly set off without delay, while the other two remained with their little flock. On taking their departure, they experienced the most agonizing sensations: partly, as they knew not what might be the issue of the journey; and partly, as they were obliged to leave their families in want of the common necessaries of life. As they travelled chiefly by land, along the banks of Lake Erie, they had to pass through numerous swamps, over large inundated plains, and through thick forests. But the most painful circumstance was, their hearing that some of the Indians, who had gone to Muskingum to fetch corn, had been murdered by the white people; and that a large body of these miscreants were marching to Sandusky, to surprise the new settlement. This report, indeed, was not correct. Shebosh, the missionary, and five of the Christian Indians were, it is true, taken prisoners at Shoenbrunn and carried to Pittsburg. The others returned safe to Sandusky, with about four hundred bushels of Indian corn, which they had gathered in the fields. But as the travellers did not hear a correct statement of these circumstances until afterwards, they suffered meanwhile the greatest anxiety and distress.

"Having arrived at Detroit, they appeared before the governor, in order to answer the accusations brought against them, of holding a correspondence [230] with the Americans, to the prejudice of the English interest. The investigation, however, was deferred till Captain Pipe, their principal accuser, should arrive. A circumstance which could not but give them much uneasiness, as he had hitherto shown himself their bitter and determined enemy. They had no friend on earth to interpose in their behalf; but they had a Friend in heaven, in whom they put their trust: nor was their confidence in Him in vain. On the day of trial, Captain Pipe, after some ceremonies had passed between him and Colonel de Peyster, respecting the scalps and prisoners which he had brought from the United States, rose and addressed the governor as follows:—'Father—You commanded us to bring the believing Indians and their teachers from the Muskingum. This has been done. When we had brought them to Sandusky, you ordered us to bring their teachers and some of their chiefs unto you. Here you see them before you. Now you may speak with them yourself, as you have desired. But I hope you will speak good words unto them: yea, I tell you, speak good words unto them; for they are my friends, and I should be sorry to see them ill used.' These last words he repeated two or three times. In reply to this speech, the governor enumerated the various complaints he had made against the brethren, and called upon him to prove that they had actually corresponded with the Americans, to the prejudice of the English. To this the chief replied, that such a thing might have happened; but they would do it no more, for they were now at Detroit. [231] The governor, justly dissatisfied with this answer, peremptorily demanded that he should give a direct reply to his question. Pipe was now greatly embarrassed; and, bending to his counsellors, asked them what he should say. But they all hung their heads in silence. On a sudden, however, he rose, and thus addressed the governor:—'I said before that such a thing might have happened; now I will tell you the truth. The missionaries are innocent. They have done nothing of themselves; what they did, they were compelled to do.' Then, smiting his breast, he added: 'I am to blame, and the chiefs who were with me. We forced them to do it when they refused;' alluding to the correspondence between the Delaware chiefs and the Americans, of which the missionaries were the innocent medium. Thus the brethren found an advocate and a friend in their accuser and enemy.

"After making some further inquiries, the governor declared, before the whole camp, that the brethren were innocent of all the charges alleged against them; that he felt great satisfaction in their endeavours to civilize and Christianize the Indians; and that he would permit them to return to their congregation without delay. He even offered them the use of his own house, in the most friendly manner; and as they had been plundered, contrary to his express command, he ordered them to be supplied with clothes, and various other articles of which they stood in need. He even bought the four watches which the savages had taken from them and sold to a trader. After experiencing [232] various other acts of kindness from him they returned to Sandusky, and were received with inexpressible joy by their families and the whole congregation."

Austin. Well, I am glad it has all ended so happily. Captain Pipe and Colonel de Peyster acted an unworthy part, to suspect the missionaries.

Brian. They did; but the colonel declared before the whole camp that they were innocent. That was making some amends for his suspicions.

Basil. Captain Pipe ought to have been ashamed of himself.

Hunter. The missionaries went through various trials, and nearly a hundred Christian Indians—men, women and children—were cruelly slaughtered; but afterwards the missions began to wear a more prosperous appearance. I have now kept you longer than usual. The next time you come here, I will finish my missionary account. Though among the tribes near the whites great changes have taken place, yet, among the Indians of the far-west, their customs are but little altered. They join in the buffalo hunt, assemble in the war-party, engage in their accustomed games, and smoke the pipe of peace, the same as ever.

Missionary and Indians.

CHAPTER XVI. [233]

In the former part of the hunter's relation, Austin Edwards and his brothers thought of little else than of bluffs and prairies, buffaloes, bears and beavers, warlike Indian chiefs and the spirit-stirring adventures of savage life; but the last visit paid to the cottage had considerably sobered their views. The hunter had gradually won his way into their affections, by contributing largely to their amusement; and he had, also, secured their respect and high opinion, by his serious remarks. They had no doubt of his being a true friend to Indians, and they had, on that account, listened the more attentively to what he had advanced on the subject of missionaries. The knowledge that they were about to hear the end of the [234] hunter's relation, though it hung a little heavy on their spirits, disposed them to seriousness and attention.

"And now," said the hunter, as soon as Austin, Brian, and Basil had seated themselves in his cottage, and requested him to continue his missionary account, "I will give you the best statement I can, in a few words, of the number of people who are employed among the Indians in the missionary cause."

Austin. Yes; we shall like to hear that very well.

Hunter. The American Board of Commissioners for Foreign Missions sustain missionary stations among the Cherokees, Choctaws, Pawnees, Oregon tribes, Sioux, Ojibbewas, Stockbridge tribe, New York tribes and the Abenaquis. There are twenty-five stations and twenty-three missionaries, three medical missionaries, three native preachers, two physicians, ten male and forty-five female assistants.

The Board of Missions connected with the Presbyterian church sustain missions among the Creeks, the Iowas and Sacs, and the Chippeways and Ottawas; three missionaries and their wives and several teachers are employed.

The missionary society of the Methodist Episcopal church have established missions among the Shawnees, Delawares, Wyandotts, Kickapoos, Pottawatomies, Choctaws, Chickasaws, Cherokees, Senecas, Creeks, Oneidas, Winnebagoes and some smaller tribes. From an old report of this [235] laborious society, 1844, I have copied a passage which I will read you:

"It is now generally conceded, by those best acquainted with the peculiarities of the Indian character, that however powerful the gospel may be, in itself, to melt and subdue the savage heart, it is indispensable, if we would secure the fruits of our missionary labours, to connect the blessings of civilization with all our Christian efforts. And we rejoice to learn, that among many of the Indian tribes the civilizing process is going on, and keeping pace with their spiritual advancement. They are turning their attention more and more to agriculture, and the various arts of civilized life. They have also established a number of schools and academies, some of which they have liberally endowed from the annuities they receive from the United States government. Some of these schools are already in successful operation, and many of the Indian youth are making rapid advancement in literary pursuits."

The Baptist Board of Missions have seven missions, embracing nineteen stations and out-stations, thirty-two missionaries and assistants, ten native preachers and assistants, fifteen organized churches and sixteen hundred professing Christians. These missionary labours are among the Ojibbewas, Ottowas, Tonewandas, Tuscaroras, Shawnees, Cherokees, Creeks and Choctaws.

The United Brethren or Moravians, and the Board of Missions of the Protestant Episcopal church, also maintain missions among the Indians. [236]

Austin. How do the missionaries preach to the Indians? Do they understand their strange language?

Hunter. Your question calls to my mind one of the most interesting and remarkable events of Indian history. I will endeavour to give you a brief account of it. I refer to the invention of an alphabet by a native Cherokee named George Guess or Guyst, who knew not how to speak English and was never taught to read English books. It was in 1824-5 that this invention began to attract considerable attention. Having become acquainted with the principle of the alphabet; viz. that marks can be made the symbols of sound; this uninstructed man conceived the notion that he could express all the syllables in the Cherokee language by separate marks, or characters.

On collecting all the syllables which, after long study and trial, he could recall to his memory, he found the number to be *eighty-two*. In order to express these, he took the letters of our alphabet for a part of them, and various modifications of our letters, with some characters of his own invention, for the rest. With these symbols he set about writing letters; and very soon a correspondence was actually maintained between the Cherokees in Wills Valley, and their countrymen beyond the Mississippi, 500 miles apart. This was done by individuals who could not speak English, and who had never learned any alphabet, except this syllabic one, which Guess had invented, taught to others, and introduced into practice. The [237] interest in this matter increased till, at length, young Cherokees travelled a great distance to be instructed in this easy method of writing and reading. In three days they were able to commence letter-writing, and return home to their native villages prepared to teach others. Either Guess himself, or some other person afterwards, discovered *four* other syllables; making all the known syllables of the Cherokee language *eighty-six*. This is a very curious fact; especially when it is considered that the language is very copious on some subjects, a single verb undergoing some thousands of inflections. All syllables in the Cherokee language end with vowels. The same is true of the language of the islanders of the Pacific ocean. But in the Choctaw language, syllables often end with consonants.

"Some months since," says a report of the Cherokee mission in 1825, "Mr. David Brown commenced the translation of the New Testament into Cherokee, with the occasional assistance of two or three of his countrymen, who are more thoroughly acquainted, than he is, with that language. Already the four Gospels are translated, and fairly copied; and if types and a press were ready, they could be immediately revised and printed and read. Extracts are now transcribed and perused by a few.

"It is manifest that such a translation must be very imperfect; but it is equally manifest that much divine truth maybe communicated by it, and probably with more accuracy than is commonly [238] done by preaching, either with an interpreter, or without one."

Another account is a little more full:

"It is well worthy of notice, that Mr. Guyst, the inventor, is a man past the middle age. He had seen books, and, I have been told, had an English spelling-book in his house; but he could not read a word in any language, nor speak the English language at all. His alphabet consists of eighty-six characters, each of which represents a syllable, with the exception of one, which has the sound of the English *s*, and is prefixed to other characters when required. These eighty-six characters are sufficient to write the language, at least intelligibly. The alphabet is thought by some of the Cherokees to need improvement; but, as it is, it is read by a very large portion of the people, though I suppose there has been no such thing as a school in which it has been taught, and it is not more than two or three years since it was invented. A few hours of instruction are sufficient for a Cherokee to learn to read his own language intelligibly. He will not, indeed, so soon be able to read *fluently*: but when he has learned to read and understand, fluency will be acquired by practice. The extent of my information will not enable me to form a probable estimate of the number in the nation who can thus read, but I am assured, by those who had the best opportunity of knowing, that there is no part of the nation where the new alphabet is not understood. That it will prevail over every other method of writing the language, there is no doubt. [239] "

Austin. Did they find the language could be easily written and printed?

Hunter. In 1828 one of the missionaries of the American Board devoted himself to the acquisition of the language, with a view to translating the Scriptures, and preparing school-books and tracts for the general instruction of the people. As he proceeded in the study of the language, he found it more and more wonderful in its structure, and the difficulties which must have attended the labour of reducing it to a system became more and more apparent.

Before this, however, the enthusiasm of the people was kindled: great numbers had learned to read; they were circulating hymns and portions of Scripture, and writing letters every day, and even procured a medal to present to the inventor, as a token of their gratitude for this wonderful method of writing their own language. They began to talk much of printing in the new and famous characters; appropriated money to procure a press and types, and anticipated with joy the printing of the Scriptures in a language they could read and understand.

At the same time the missionaries to the Choctaws were reducing their language to a system. One of them collected more than 3000 words, arranged according to the subjects to which they refer, which he translated into English. Ten hymns were also translated into Choctaw, and a spelling-book prepared in the same language. [240]

Austin. But let us hear what became of the Guyst's Cherokee alphabet. As that was an invention of his own, it seems very wonderful.

Hunter. I will tell you. In the summer or fall of 1827, there was an examination of one of the Cherokee mission schools, on which occasion one of the chiefs made an address in the Cherokee language, of which the following is a translation.

"Dear children:—I often speak to you, and encourage you to continue in the pursuit of useful knowledge; such knowledge as will be for your own good, and that of your own country. You are engaged in a good thing. I am always pleased to see the progress you are making in learning. I feel that much depends on you. On you depends the future welfare of your country.

"When I was young there were no schools among us. No one to teach us such learning as you are now obtaining. My lot was quite different from yours. You have here many advantages. Improve them. Pursue the paths of virtue and knowledge. Some of your fathers, who first agreed for the teachers to come among us, are now no more. They are gone.

"It is now some years since a school was established in Creekpath, your native place. I myself aided to build the first schoolhouse. At first the children did not learn very fast. But now, since the establishment of a school at this place, they are doing much better. I have reason to believe you are learning as fast as might be expected. Some of you have been in school five [241] years, and some not so long. You have now acquired considerable knowledge. By-and-by you will have more. This gives me great satisfaction.

Remember that the whites are near us. With them we have constant intercourse; and you must be sensible that, unless you can speak their language, read and write as they do, they will be able to cheat you and trample upon your rights. Be diligent, therefore, in your studies, and let nothing hinder you from them. Do not quarrel with each other. Aid one another in your useful employ; obey your teachers, and walk in the way they tell you."

In November, after this speech was delivered, a fount of types in the new Cherokee alphabet was shipped from Boston to the Cherokee nation: and from an account published at the time, I take a few sentences.

"The press will be employed in printing the New Testament and other portions of the Bible, and school-books in the Cherokee language, and such other books in Cherokee or English as will tend to diffuse knowledge through the nation. A prospectus has also been issued for a newspaper, entitled the *Cherokee Phœnix*, to be printed partly in Cherokee, and partly in English; the first number of which is expected to appear early in January. All this has been done by order of the Cherokee government, and at their expense. They have also hired a printer to superintend the printing office, to whom they give $400 a year, and another printer to whom they give $300. [242] Mr. Elias Boudinot, who was educated, in part, at the Foreign Mission School, then established in Cornwall, (Conn.,) was appointed editor, with a yearly salary of $300.

"Among the Cherokees, then, we are to see the first printing-press ever owned and employed by any nation of the aborigines of this continent; the first effort at writing and printing in characters of their own; the first newspaper, and the first book printed among themselves; the first editor; and the first well organized system for securing a general diffusion of knowledge among the people. Among the Cherokees, also, we see established the first regularly elective government, with the legislative, judicial, and executive branches distinct; with the safeguards of a written constitution and trial by jury. Here, also, we see first the Christian religion recognised and protected by the government; regular and exemplary Christian churches; and flourishing schools extensively established, and, in many instances, taught by native Cherokees."

Brian. I suppose, by this time, they have a great many books printed, and more than one newspaper.

Hunter. Alas, poor fellows! they have had something very different to think about since the times I have been speaking of. I cannot make you understand all the particulars. But the government of the state within whose bounds the Indian country lay, wished to have the Indians under their control; while the Indians considered [243] themselves, and had always been treated by the United States government as independent nations or communities. Treaties were made with them just as with foreign nations. There were difficulties on every side. A proposition was made to them, to sell their lands to the United States, and remove to a country beyond the Mississippi. Some of the tribes were in favour of this, and some were opposed to it. The state government became more and more urgent for their removal, and at last effectual measures were adopted for this purpose, and the Cherokees and other tribes were driven from their homes, which were now becoming the abodes of civilization and comfort and Christian love, and were compelled to find a new residence in the far, far distant West. It is a melancholy and reproachful chapter in our history as a nation; and we have reason to fear that a day of retribution is at hand, if, indeed, it is not now upon us. There is a just God, who plucks up and destroys even the mighty nations of the earth; and, in every period of the world, his power to visit their iniquities has been exhibited.

Austin. And have all efforts for their improvement been given up?

Hunter. O, no. As I told you just now, several interesting and prosperous missions are established among them in their new abode; and so lately as the years 1843-4, the sum of $300 was appropriated by the American Bible Society, towards printing portions of the New Testament in the Dakota tongue, for the use of the Sioux. [244] And the same blessed volume is now in the course of publication at the Bible Society's house in New York, in the language of the Ojibbewas. This is a large tribe, and their tongue is understood by several of the neighbouring tribes. It is hoped that the possession of the gospel of peace by the Sioux and Ojibbewas, in their respective tongues, will produce a more pacific spirit between these two hostile tribes. To this end Christians should pray that the Scriptures of truth may be accompanied by the Spirit of truth; that they may bring forth the fruits of holiness; and that the remnant of the tribes may all be brought to the knowledge of the Saviour.

There are many obstacles to this most desirable event. The wars that break out unexpectedly among the tribes, the reverence entertained for superstitious customs, their removals from one place to another, the natural indolence of Indians, and their love of spirituous liquors, given by white men in order to deceive them; these and other causes are always at work, operating against the efforts of the missionary. I might, it is true, give you more instances than I have done of an encouraging kind, respecting the Indians generally. [6]

[6] The reader is referred to a memoir of Catharine Brown, a converted Cherokee girl, (written by the Rev. Dr. Anderson, and published by the *American Sunday-school Union,*) for one of the most interesting exhibitions of the influence of the Gospel upon the human heart, as well as for a very correct and gratifying account of missionary labour and success among untutored Indians. [245]

But, perhaps, it will be better now to sum up the account by saying, the missionary is at work among them with some degree of success; and though, from the remoteness of many of the tribes, their strong attachment to the superstitions of their forefathers, and other causes already alluded to, the progress of Christianity is necessarily slow, there is no doubt that it will ultimately prevail; the promise has gone forth, and will be fulfilled; the heathen will be the inheritance of the Redeemer, and the uttermost parts of the earth will be his possession. He who has clothed the arm of the red man with strength, shod his feet with swiftness, and filled his heart with courage, will, in due time, subdue his cruelty and revenge; open his eyes to discern the wondrous things of God's holy law; dispose his mind to acknowledge the Lord of life and glory, and make him willing to receive the gospel of the Redeemer.

THE END.

PUBLICATIONS OF THE M. E. CHURCH, SOUTH.

THE ART OF PRINTING. Edited by Thomas O. Summers, D.D. 18mo., pp. 185. Price 30 cts.

This volume traces the art preservative of all arts from its rude beginnings to its present approximation to perfection. It has engravings representing presses, etc.

A TREATISE ON SECRET AND SOCIAL PRAYER. By Richard Treffry. 18mo., pp. 215. Price 35 cts.

A very serviceable book.

METHODISM; or, Christianity in Earnest.

SABBATH-SCHOOL OFFERING; or, True Stories and Poems.

THE DAY-SPRING; or, Light to them that sit in Darkness.

The foregoing three volumes are interesting little books, from the pen of Mrs. M. Martin, of South Carolina. They are composed of Sketches, Incidents, Poems, etc., beautifully illustrated and neatly printed. Price, respectively, 30, 30, and 25 cts.

JERUSALEM, ANCIENT AND MODERN. Two vols. Price 60 cts.

Excellent books, embellished with elegant steel engravings.

THE PALM TRIBES—LIFE OF CYRUS—LIFE OF SIR ISAAC NEWTON—SWITZERLAND—IONA—MONEY—THE INQUISITION.

These volumes belong to a series of nearly uniform size, written by some of the first pens of the age. In every one of them a vast amount of useful information is presented in a short compass. They are of that class desiderated by Dr. Arnold—"I never wanted articles on religious subjects half so much as articles on common subjects, written with a decidedly religious turn." They are valuable additions to Sunday-school and family libraries, with special reference to which they have been carefully revised by the Editor. They are sold at 30 cts. each. London in the Olden Times, and more than thirty others, belong to this series.

VARIATIONS OF POPERY. By Samuel Edgar, D.D. 8vo., $1 25.

A masterly work.

VOLCANOES. Price 30 cts.

THE LIFE OF THE REV. JOHN W. DE LA FLECHERE Compiled from the Narrative of the Rev. Mr. Wesley; the Biographical Notes of the Rev. Mr. Gilpin, from his own Letters, and other authentic Documents, many of which were never before published. By Joseph Benson. Price 60 cts.

THE LIFE OF MRS. MARY FLETCHER, Consort and Relict of Rev. John Fletcher, Vicar of Madeley, Salop. Compiled from her Journal, and other authentic Documents. By Henry Moore. Price 60 cts.

Cheap and convenient editions of these two Methodist classics.

STORIES FOR VILLAGE LADS. By the Author of "Stories of Schoolboys," "Frank Harrison," etc. Price 35 cts.

STORIES OF SCHOOLBOYS. By the Author of "Stories for Village Lads." Price 30 cts.

Those "lads" and "boys" are English; but we can find a great many like them in the United States, though one seldom meets with such capital stories as these *for* them and *of* them.

ST. PETER'S CHAIN OF CHRISTIAN VIRTUES. By the Rev. C. D. Oliver, of the Alabama Conference. Price 40 cents.

An edifying treatise, based on 2 Pet. i. 5-7.

CHRISTIAN THEOLOGY: By Adam Clarke, LL.D., F.A.S.

Selected from his published and unpublished Writings, and systematically arranged. With a Life of the Author. By Samuel Dunn. Price 75 cts.

A carefully revised edition of this great work.

THE GREAT SUPPER NOT CALVINISTIC; being a Reply to the Rev. Dr. Fairchild's Discourses on the Parable of the Great Supper. By Leroy M. Lee, D.D. Price 50 cts.

There is no mincing the matter in this sturdy volume. Evenhanded justice is dealt out to Dr. Fairchild, with his aiders and abettors; and the gospel of the grace of God is triumphantly defended from their Calvinistic imputations.